The Way of the Woods

The Way of the Woods

JOURNEYS THROUGH AMERICAN FORESTS

Linda Underhill

Oregon State University Press
Corvallis

The paper in this book meets the guidelines for permanence and durability of the Committee on Production Guidelines for Book Longevity of the Council on Library Resources and the minimum requirements of the American National Standard for Permanence of Paper for Printed Library Materials Z39.48-1984.

Library of Congress Cataloging-in-Publication Data
Underhill, Linda.
  The way of the woods : journeys through America's forests / Linda Underhill.
    p. cm.
  ISBN 978-0-87071-568-6 (alk. paper)
  1. Forests and forestry--United States. 2. Forest ecology--United States. I. Title.
  SD143.U43 2009
  508.31520973--dc22

                                    2008055807

First published in 2009 by Oregon State University Press
Printed in the United States of America

 Oregon State University Press
121 The Valley Library
Corvallis OR 97331-4501
541-737-3166 • fax 541-737-3170
http://oregonstate.edu/dept/press

This book is for Bill

Contents

Preface

In my imagination, I can picture it, a continent covered with all types of trees: the shadowy spruces lining the shores, the mighty pines crowning the hillsides, the ancient chestnuts populating the plateaus, the oaks rising on the cliffs overlooking the gorges, the sugar maples blazing red and gold on an autumn morning, the hemlocks bent green and graceful over silver streams, the beeches, the birches, the aspens, the tamaracks, the sequoias and the cedars, the redwoods and the firs. Like a bird soaring over the treetops I travel, my eye on the vast green world below me.

I can picture it because I have seen a small portion of what remains. "The forests of America, however slighted by man, must have been a delight to God," said John Muir, "for they were the best he ever planted." No one knew our forests better than Muir, who walked the continent tirelessly. I have walked only a few short miles in comparison to his thousands. As an ordinary person with no experience in backpacking or bushwhacking, I often wondered what I was doing out in the woods. Yet for three years, whenever I could find the time and the money and whenever I could manage to get away, I left my home in order to see for myself what remains of some of the extraordinary environments of our nation's forests and woodlands.

It is incredible, in ways, that anything at all remains of our forests. They were indeed slighted by man, who conquered them as if they were the enemy. It was almost too late when we realized that *we* were the enemy. The first European settlers cleared the trees to make farms. Then the loggers came, felling the largest and the oldest trees from coast to coast and sending them to the sawmills. We used our forests to build what we called our United States of America, with our homes, our factories, our schools, our churches, our railroads, our telephone poles, our tables and chairs and baseball bats, all made of trees. Our finest trees were sawed up into boards, chopped up into toothpicks, and ground up into pulp.

Some voices were raised in defense of trees. In 1850 Susan Fenimore Cooper lamented the loss of the forest outside her village in upstate New York. A few of the old trees remained, but "their nearer brethren have all been swept away, and these are left in isolated company," she wrote in her book *Rural Hours*. She urged her fellow citizens to pause and consider how long it would take to reproduce the forests they were so eager to clear away.

Fifty years later, in his essay "The American Forests," Muir echoed her sentiments, saying, "Any fool can destroy trees. They cannot run away; and if they could, they would still be destroyed—chased and hunted down as long as fun or a dollar could be got out of their bark hides." Muir advocated federal protection for our most extraordinary trees in the form of national parks like Yosemite. Today, some people think the forests in these protected places are in danger of being loved to death by tourists, but at least they still exist.

The same cannot be said for the great chestnut forests of the Appalachian plateau, which succumbed to a blight introduced from Asia on imported nursery stock. Or the mighty white pine forests of western Pennsylvania, most of which succumbed to the saw. By the early twentieth century, cut-over, barren hillsides were the norm. But when I was a child growing up in Pittsburgh in the 1950s, an extraordinary metamorphosis was taking place. All around me, hillsides that had been stripped bare of their trees were growing green once more. All I knew, when my family moved to the suburbs, was that there were trees everywhere I looked, and I spent many carefree hours playing in the woods around our home. Trees were my constant companions, and while I understood little about ecology, I loved the green, protective presence of trees, their invitations to climb and reach, their shapely beauty, and their habit of making music in the wind. A landscape without trees will always be unwelcoming to me. I don't want to live without trees.

Today, thanks in part to a changing economy, along with a growing environmental awareness on the part of American citizens, our woodlands are green once more. Despite the destruction of the great clear-cut logging era of the late nineteenth and early twentieth centuries, despite the damage done by blights and plagues of predator insects, despite commercial development and acid rain and global warming, some riches remain, and they are as difficult to resist as ever. Profiteers still want to cut down the little that remains of our ancient forests. I wanted not the logs, however, but the sight and sound of our forests and woodlands, wherever I could find them, in national parks, in state parks, in nature preserves, in forests owned by the federal government and forests owned by private citizens. This book represents a little of what I saw, and a little of what there is to learn about our native forests and the dangers they still face.

As "civilized" people living in cities and towns, we often forget that without forests, we literally cannot breathe, because trees take carbon dioxide out of the air and convert it to oxygen. Forests filter air and light, cleaning and cooling the atmosphere and sequestering carbon to combat global climate change. Trees hold the ground against erosion with their roots and build up the soil with nitrogen from their own decaying leaves and wood, giving life for more life. Microorganisms we don't even know about yet live in that soil, keeping it alive and fertile for the trees, which keep the planet alive and breathing for us.

We also rely on forests for clean drinking water. As enlightened communities all over the world now realize, preserving forested watersheds is much more efficient and cost effective than building billion-dollar water-treatment plants. A forest is like a gigantic sponge; trees absorb rainwater and release it slowly into the ground, preventing erosion and keeping water available and flowing at a steady pace. In a wild forest, where pesticides, herbicides, and fertilizers aren't in use and there is no industrial waste, the water is clean and free of pollutants. Fresh, clean water is something we all take for granted. But if we don't protect our forests, we may find that the tap runs dry.

On a purely practical level, forests provide us with wood to build homes. If we choose to build unwisely, we will have less and less of the best building material as time goes by. If we learn to practice sustainable logging and limit our use of forest products to what we really need, the riches our forests contain will remain for future generations.

On a profoundly spiritual level, forests also provide us with a glimpse of paradise on earth. Home to a myriad of flora and fauna, a healthy forest is one of the glories of creation. To go as far as the forest is to confront the ultimate reality—to remember that even while we live in cities and towns, we too have a place in the natural world. Our relationship with forests is an ancient one, and no less sacred today than ever before in our history. Our first sanctuaries were groves of towering trees. When we go as far as the forest now, we remember our deep and lasting connection with a forested environment. And thanks to the "greening of America," forests are not out of reach for most Americans. Many of our cities and towns have access to nature preserves, state parks, or national forests with well-developed trail systems where we can renew that connection and enjoy its benefits: a sense of belonging in the natural world, an understanding of the interconnectedness of all living things, and as Rachel Carson said, a sense of wonder at the miracle of life in all its forms as an antidote against alienation from the true sources of our strength.

Each of the forests and woodlands I have visited has its own unique character and form, each has a special story to tell, and each reveals its own truth about the nature of life on earth. Each of the places I visited also taught me something specific about forest ecology. I learned about the unique character of old-growth forests, the value found in the "urban forest" of trees growing in cities and towns, the ways that nature controls her own in the forest's web of life, the importance of fire to forest ecosystems, the critical role that forests play in combating global climate change, and the wisdom of preserving undeveloped wilderness areas and wildlife habitats in our forests. I learned about the place of forests in our cultural heritage and our spiritual beliefs. I witnessed the cycles of life and death in the forest as the wheel of the seasons turns throughout the year.

I learned that while many of our forests are green again, they are also under assault wherever their natural ability to regenerate is threatened and wherever human influences have caused imbalances—tears in the fragile web of life. Blights and pests introduced from overseas are killing some of our most beautiful native trees. In many places, an out-of-control deer herd is obliterating the seedlings that would bring new life to forests. Global climate change and acid rain threaten to destroy the conditions necessary for maintaining healthy forests. Our federal government has slashed conservation budgets, and incredibly, even advocated selling the land in national forests to developers. Curiously, the element we often think most destructive—fire—is in ways more friend than foe. After over a hundred years of fire suppression in the United States, ecologists now recognize that fire is a necessary element in a forest's natural cycle of life, death, and regeneration. Learning to see fire as a friend is just one of the challenges we face at a time when what we do now may decide the fate of our forests for centuries to come.

I am not a rugged person, and in the beginning, I expected to be cold, hungry, tired, and foot sore on my wandering hours in the woods. I was surprised to find that as soon as one trip was over, I could hardly wait for the next one to begin. Thanks to the expert guidance of modern-day Druids who seemed to pop up magically whenever I needed them, I was never lost. Immersed in the shapes, the sounds, the color and light of a forest, what Susan Fenimore Cooper called the *wild dignity of form* in trees that have lived for centuries, I found myself connected to the joy of being alive. Walking in an old-growth forest, I was surrounded by the eternal mysteries of life, death, and transformation. In the forest, it was going on all around me every moment, this process of growth and decay, reaching and falling, giving and taking away. I often felt that I was inside the mind of the universe. I have stood inside a few of the great cathedrals people have built—St. Paul's Cathedral in London, Notre Dame in Paris, St. Peter's Basilica in Rome. These structures are all beautiful, they are all inspiring, and while they are all great works of art and testaments to the faith of those who built them, none of them compares with the beauty and majesty of a forest, where the trees are alive and reaching for the sky, where the light is always changing, where wind, rain, fire, and ice are all celebrants in the daily liturgy of life on planet Earth. The sight of trees, the sound of them, the scent of them, the *presence* of what poet e.e. cummings called the "leaping greenly spirits of trees" affirmed my kinship with all that is wild, all that is real, all, as cummings said, "which is natural which is infinite which is yes." In the forest, I often experienced what perceptual psychologist Laura Sewall has called "an ecstatic liberation of the senses." It was very much like being in love.

It has often been said that we only save what we love, and we only love what we know. If we do what we can to protect our native forests at this moment in history, we may be able to preserve what exists today for future generations, so that they too can know and love the leaping greenly spirits of trees.

At home again, I look out at the trees in my yard, tall old spruces and pines and hemlocks, evergreen and pointing towards the sky. Winter is coming, and tonight I will sleep in my comfortable bed while the furnace warms the room. But I carry the forest within me now, a leaf-fringed world of bark and branch, mud and moss, river and rock. I hear the owl's voice calling from the ancient pines, and the deer's hoof stepping across the stream. The path lies before me. There is still time.

CHAPTER ONE
Old Growth

As I drive towards the Pennsylvania border from my home in western New York on a cool, bright day in May, a few low clouds wipe the sky and send shadows streaming over the hillsides. Hawks float above me, surveying the treetops. Nearer the ground, yellow and black tiger swallowtail butterflies struggle in the slipstream caused by my car. By the roadside, buttercups lift fragile yellow petals to the sun.

I turn off the freeway in Olean and drive south on Route 646 toward Bradford, Pennsylvania. The hills here are green as only a wet eastern spring can make them—all shades of green, fresh and unfaded green, alive and growing green, the green of the eastern forest approaching the summer of the year and the longest day of light.

Near the crest of the hill between Olean and Bradford, I cross the state line into Pennsylvania. This is the state where I was born, so in a way I am not leaving home—I am coming home. I descend the hill on a two-lane road winding through woodlands of evergreens, oak, and maple. At the base of the hill I reach the outskirts of Bradford, where large brick houses and manicured lawns have taken the place of the woods. Turning onto the freeway, I see the oil refineries outside of town making an incongruous contrast with the green hillsides surrounding them, a reminder that the lumber boom was barely over here when the oil boom got its start.

A half an hour's drive later I pick up Route 66 in Kane. It is Memorial Day weekend, and as I pass the Forest Lawn cemetery outside of Kane, I see a crew of men walking among the tombstones, placing American flags at the graves of veterans. A few miles further down the road is a sign that proclaims I am entering the Allegheny National Forest. But I already know I am in the land of the tall trees. They tower over the road, a shadowy realm of oak, beech, birch, hemlock, and a few white pine. Beneath the trees, among mossy green rocks, ferns are frothing.

Two hundred years ago, this forest was dominated by the great white pine. A truly northern tree, white pine actually likes the bitterly cold winters as well as the warm, sweet summers of the Appalachian plateau. Young white pine have a bushy shape, but as they grow tall over the years, they acquire a more architectural form, as if they are building living structures of their own design. Mature trees have a layered outline, their branches forming platforms like the various levels of a pagoda, their long, soft needles growing in clusters on whorled branches. After two hundred years, the bark on the tall old trees becomes roughly corrugated, ruffled with lichen and moss. I see only a few white pine growing in the forest by the roadside now. But once, Pennsylvania and most of New York was one great stand of virgin white pine—"Pines and pines and the shadow of pines as far as the eye can see," as the poet Robert Service wrote. This pine forest was so vast that it was said a squirrel could spend an entire lifetime traveling from one tree to another without ever visiting the ground. An exaggeration, perhaps, intended to lure settlers to the lumber industry, but the image conjures something of what this forest must have looked like before European settlers arrived. Despite the devastation wrought by the clear-cutting of timber in the nineteenth century, despite the cutting of forests to clear the way for farms, mines, factories, railroads, and highways, a few pockets of old-growth pine remain, glimpses of the forest primeval, and I am on my way to visit one of these places, in Cook Forest, by the banks of the Clarion River.

John Cook came to Western Pennsylvania in 1826, built a cabin near the river, and used water power to drive his sawmills. Like hundreds of other enterprising settlers, he saw the great trees as a treasure to be claimed, a commodity to be sold. White pine had already made more than one fortune. It is the first of the trees discussed in Donald Peattie's books on American trees, and Peattie calls it "the first gold that the New England settlers struck." In colonial times, the tall, straight trunks of the virgin trees were cut to make ships' masts for the British Navy. Britain had already cut down most of its own forests; now, it was eagerly importing lumber from the new world. American colonists were just as eager to conquer the forests, clearing trees to make room for farms and towns. Once the colonies won their independence, Peattie says, white pine literally built the new United States. Lumber from virgin white pine was easy to cut and mill, yet it retained a strength making it ideal for everything from roof shingles to doors to bobsleds. Its smooth, straight grain made it perfect for the heddles on a weaver's loom, so in a sense, white pine even helped to clothe the new citizens of the United States. As the nation expanded west, a hungry America devoured one stand of fine virgin timber after another in what must have seemed an unlimited supply.

But of course it was not. The practices of the timber industry in the nineteenth century took into account only the immediate commercial value of the timber, cutting the best trees as quickly as possible and moving on to the next place, with no thought of replanting for the future. In the 1920s, when most of the nation's virgin white pine was gone, conservationists finally raised public awareness to save the small percentage of virgin forest left, creating protected areas like Cook Forest State Park. Places like this one are all that remain of the once mighty pine forests of the Appalachian Plateau. Cook Forest provides a glimpse of what the white pine forests of North America looked like two hundred years ago.

The Clarion River curls through the eastern edge of the park, and the first indication that I have arrived are the landings where stacks of canoes await those who want to travel as the Seneca Nation once did, by river, creek, and stream. Heading towards the park entrance on Route 36, I pass trading posts and cabins rapidly filling up for the holiday weekend. Unlike many parks around the country, there is no gate here where I must stop and pay a fee to enter. But there are plenty of places to spend money. Besides the trading posts selling Indian-inspired T-shirts, moccasins, and tooled leather wallets, there are a swimming pool, bridle trails, and the Sawmill Craft Center and Theater offering classes in wood carving, painting, drawing, and basket weaving, along with summer theater productions like "Godspell" and "Arsenic and Old Lace."

I avoid all these enterprises and drive down a tree-lined road to the Environmental Learning Center, a log cabin built in 1934 by Roosevelt's

Civil Conservation Corps. Behind the cabin, the Longfellow Trail leads up into the old-growth forest. I park my car in the lot and find a picnic table where I can sit and study my trail map. With a half-dozen other people, I am waiting for Dale Luthringer, who will lead a hike into the "Forest Cathedral" area straddling the boundary between Forest and Clarion counties on my map. We are hoping to see some of the oldest and largest white pine trees still standing in the eastern United States.

Eight thousand acres have been set aside in Cook Forest, fifteen hundred of them considered old-growth forest. They are neither pristine nor undisturbed. Some of them have been logged; in some of them, fallen trees have been removed. But according to Bruce Kershner, author of a number of books about the Northeast's oldest forests, if trees at least a hundred fifty years old dominate a forest, then it can be called old growth. In his *Sierra Club Guide to the Ancient Forests of the Northeast,* which I've also brought with me today, Kershner calls Cook Forest "The gem of the Northeast's old-growth woodlands," and says the age of the trees here ranges from two hundred fifty to four hundred years old. On inaccessible slopes and steep ravines the loggers couldn't reach, or in places the timber barons set aside to enjoy as artifacts of the forest's beauty, these bits of old growth still exist here and there. John Cook saved a few acres of the most beautiful forest around the spot where he and his family lived. I wonder if he realized that in doing so he was actually preserving history.

Luthringer is late, so I explore a little way up the gently sloping hill behind the cabin. Standing here are hundred-year-old hemlocks and pines, trees allowed to grow up after the loggers left, and the ground beneath them is brown with their fallen needles. On an old stump, a vivid orange fungus is growing in the shape of plump scallop shells still holding some of last week's rain in shallow fonts. I am staring at this odd fungus when I notice a figure in an odd costume of blue britches and a blue tasseled cap striding up to the cabin. It's Luthringer, looking a bit embarrassed to be dressed this way, fresh from a re-enactment of a French and Indian War battle being commemorated this weekend. I hurry over to meet the group gathering around him as he explains that the re-enactors weren't permitted modern wristwatches, so he's still on eighteenth-century time. In his long black woolen socks, buckled shoes, blousy white cotton shirt, and blue cap embellished with a tassel and a gold fleur de lis, he certainly looks like someone from another century—but which one, I'm not entirely sure.

While we try to ignore his vaguely elf-like costume, Luthringer instructs us in the differences between the white pine and the hemlock, to be sure we can identify them later. I already know that the white pine has clusters of five long, fine needles grouped together, while the hemlock has short, flat needles growing straight out from the branch of the tree. Luthringer points out that the white pine, once it has lived a long time, will tend to lose its lower branches more than the hemlock. We test our knowledge on a few of the trees around the cabin, identifying them as either pine or hemlock. Then we head up the trail behind the cabin and into the forest.

Luthringer looks like he weighs no more than a hundred sixty pounds, and he walks quickly, setting a brisk pace. He scrambles nimbly up a bank to stand next to an enormous hemlock that seems to be growing right out of a large boulder on the bank, and waits for our group to catch up with him and gather around.

"The Cook Forest is a very special area that's been set aside to see how an old-growth forest works," Luthringer says, describing it as a kind of "working laboratory" for studying the unique ecosystem created by trees that are left alone for hundreds of years. But Cook Forest is far from being a tree museum; this area has often seen nature's fury. Luthringer says a great fire must have raged here in the mid 1600s, creating the open space that allowed white pine to germinate and grow; more recently, windstorms leveled some trees on this hillside in the mid 1950s. Lightning has left swirling burn marks on the bark of some living trees, and struck others dead. Still, Cook Forest has more 150-feet-tall white pine than any other site in the Northeast. A recent survey found fifty at that height, and twenty-six more reaching 160 feet or higher. There are at least four trees measuring 170 feet, and one—the Longfellow Pine—over 180 feet tall.

Luthringer shows us how to identify the oldest trees, with their deeply furrowed bark, their "balding" patterns where the bark has worn away, their twisted arms, and their top branches growing into "antlered" or "staghorn" shapes after the tall, exposed tips of the evergreen trees break off. He tells us to notice the special features of an old-growth forest, which we can see all around us. There are large, standing dead trees known as "snags," and other large, moss-covered trees lying on the ground. Some of these fallen giants have been sectioned and moved from the trail so that we can make our way into the forest, but other than that they remain, protecting and nourishing the soil and providing shelter for spiders, salamanders, and toads. We see living trees that seem to be planted in rows, trees that have actually sprung up along the length of a fallen tree that acted as a "nurse" a century or more ago and since then has rotted away and disappeared while the new trees flourished. And there are "hummock hollow" depressions created by the places where a fallen tree's roots have pulled earth from the ground. An old-growth forest also has multiple canopy layers, as some trees grow higher and taller than the others, which struggle in their shade.

Compared to tree plantations or woodlands managed for growing a certain kind of timber, the old-growth forest is an incoherent prayer, devout but disorganized, oblivious to any demands but its own growth and decay. This sacred chaos holds the key to natural processes scientists are eager to study, but there are few places left where people have not already altered their rhythms or otherwise destroyed the evidence of creation at work. The valuable timber in old-growth forests, where trees grow hundreds of feet tall and many feet around, has proved irresistible to those who know the price such wood can bring. But an old-growth forest also offers something less easy to price in the marketplace. It invites us to witness the miracle of creation and change the way we look at our own short lives. The tall trees inspire a reverence equal to any of our own great cathedrals, and they belong only to themselves. Chopping down old-growth trees and hauling them away seems akin to scattering the stones of the Cathedral of Notre Dame and selling them off as souvenirs.

The Forest Cathedral is aptly named; primitive people thought such places sanctuaries, homes for what they knew was holy. The tall pillars of the cathedrals we build with stone are interpretations of

6

these ancient groves of trees reaching for the sky. The link between trees and a concept of the sacred is something we should not take for granted. "We should be clear about what happens when we destroy the living forms of this planet," says Thomas Berry in *The Dream of the Earth*. "The first consequence is that we destroy modes of divine presence. If we have a wonderful sense of the divine, it is because we live amid such awesome magnificence. If we have refinement of emotion and sensitivity, it is because of the delicacy, the fragrance, and indescribable beauty of song and music and rhythmic movement in the world about us." In other words, would we have the music of Bach, Beethoven, or Mozart without the "divine presence" of forests such as this? Would we have the temples of ancient Greece, the Gothic cathedrals of Europe, the painting and sculpture of the Renaissance, or the lyric poetry of the Romantics, without the inspiration of natural forms? Surely we would not have the photographs of Ansel Adams, his grand Sierra vistas, or the poetry of Basho, his sense of wonder at the daily miracles of the natural world.

> *Spring rain—*
> *beneath the trees,*
> *a crystal stream.*

When we destroy an old-growth forest we also destroy our sense of time. Leading us to a rocky grove on the slope of a hill, Luthringer stops and stands smiling amidst a number of enormously tall white pines with platy, furrowed bark. "We're in an area now that hasn't been logged before," he says as we gather around him. He informs us that somewhere right on this trail, or within twenty feet of it, is the largest tree in the forest. He challenges us to identify it by standing next to it or pointing.

As the group scatters, I look around and spot one very tall pine growing on the slope beneath the trail, some fifteen feet away. At first glance, it doesn't seem as old as some of the other trees with their furrowed bark, but as I tilt my head back to take its measure, I judge its trunk to be taller than that of the others growing around us, and it also has the distinctly "antlered" top of an ancient tree that has lost its pointed top. I stand looking at it doubtfully a while and finally decide it will be my choice as the other hikers in our group take up positions next to trees growing farther up the slope.

"Are you ready?" Luthringer asks, his brown eyes darting among us. Not waiting for a reply, he eliminates two trees in the grove where we are standing—one chosen by a stocky, dark-haired man wearing jeans and a white T-shirt, and another chosen by a woman dressed all in brown, as if she is trying to blend into the bark of the surrounding trees. Looking at trees upslope from us chosen by a tall, skinny young man and his girlfriend, Luthringer shakes his head. "Those are very big trees, but they're not the biggest," he says. I point silently to my choice below the trail, where no one else has looked, and he nods, confirming my pick. "That's the one," he says.

I have found the Longfellow Pine, the tallest tree in the northeastern United States. Twenty-first-century scientists who track tall trees often use high-tech global positioning system instruments employing laser range finders and a calculator to do trigonometry functions to measure the height of trees this large. But last year, Will Blozan of the Eastern Native Tree Society used a much more old-fashioned method. He simply climbed the tree and dropped a tape measure to a colleague standing below him on the ground. The tree measured 181 feet and 5 inches—taller than a twenty-story building—and Luthringer estimates that it is somewhere between 225 and 250 years old. "This is a very unique tree," he says. Growing down on the steep slope of the hill, maybe it had to reach higher to find the sunlight it needed for the magic of photosynthesis. Or maybe it benefited from a supply of water there. A spring trickling by at the base of the slope might have given it the advantage over the other trees. Now, looking at a tree like this, with just a little imagination, we are seeing living history. In the mid 1700s, just about when the Seneca Indians teamed up with the French to fight the British for control of this land of rich forests and streams, a seedling sprouted here and began to grow, gripping the hillside with its roots, raising a few fine fronds of pale green needles. While the French lost to the British, and Fort Duquesne became Fort Pitt, while William Penn signed treaties with the native people and established the colony of Penn's Woods, while generations of settlers lived and died and the colonies won their independence, the pine tree grew. It grew while a million other white pine all over western Pennsylvania were cut and floated down the river to Pittsburgh to be sold for their lumber. It survived a hundred winters, a hundred years of wind and rain, storm and sleet, ice and snow.

Still another hundred years have passed, and the generation of Americans who fought on the beaches of Normandy is dying now, but the tree still lives. Oblivious to the changing fortunes of commerce and war, it grows, not in competition for the status we have conferred on it as a "champion tree," but in the slow yet fierce competition all trees engage in—the one for space, and light.

There is a different kind of light in the old-growth forest. Filtered through treetops, reaching the ground here and there to gleam on an emerald moss or the delicate green fronds of a fern, the light here is quietly diffused. There is a stillness that is very like enchantment. The Wild Wood and the Black Forest are the domain of dreams, places where we imagine spirits roam in the twilight world of the shadows beneath the trees. Going as far as the forest, we leave behind the ordered human world, giving up what we think we control. Here, there are greater and older forces at work—wind, water, fire, and sun, the slow turning of the Earth in space, the quickening of life, the silent sprouting of a seed that will become a tree destined to live two hundred years or more.

These are forces we would do well to understand, or at least learn to appreciate. The old-growth forest has its own mysterious logic, its own cosmic sense of time, its own magnificent habit of being, and without interference, it produces its own unique variety of life. Mosses and lichens, mushrooms and ferns, mice and moles and those that prey on them—like owls—all make old-growth forests like this one their home in a web of life that reaches far beyond the forest and is constantly threatened by the "progress" of industrial development.

Monarch butterflies travel three thousand miles from the Northern Hemisphere to take refuge each winter in the evergreen forests of the Biosphere Reserve west of Mexico City. Tourists who have never known the bleak poverty of the native people who live there flock to the area in spring to see the butterflies. But once the butterflies leave and the tourists pack their bags, illegal loggers move in to cut down the trees in this ten-thousand-year-old forest of pine and Oyamel fir—by some estimates, taking as many as seventy trees a day. Armed loggers have attacked the poorly staffed Mexican police charged with guarding the area, threatened local communities, and offered money to peasants who have few other ways to earn a living. They have even assaulted journalists investigating the conflict. In some areas, civilian patrols guard the forest. But the World Wildlife Fund reports that forty percent of the butterfly reserve has already been destroyed.

In our own Pacific Northwest, the diminutive spotted owl has become a symbol of the conflicts between environmentalists and the timber industry. Declared an endangered species in 1991, the northern spotted owl makes the old-growth forests of Washington and Oregon its home. Under the Endangered Species Act, that habitat was declared off-limits to loggers. A "War in the Woods" ensued, with timber companies filing lawsuits against the government, environmentalists chaining themselves to trees, and angry loggers decrying the loss of their livelihood. For the past seventeen years, the battle over old growth, jobs, and the spotted owl has continued to rage.

We may think we could live without owls or monarch butterflies, but we literally cannot live without the forests that support them. Forests are sometimes called "the lungs of the earth," because trees take carbon dioxide and convert it to the oxygen we breathe. In an old-growth forest, the multiple layers of canopy filter air and light, cleaning and cooling the atmosphere. Trees hold the ground against erosion with their roots and build up the soil with nitrogen from their own decaying leaves and wood as a forest grows old, giving life for more life. Disturbing an old-growth forest to harvest its valuable timber may provide a livelihood for some people in the short run, but if it is done without thought for the value old growth provides, it destroys the cycles that keep the forest viable in the long run.

And could we live without enchantment? The old-growth forest is both a laboratory for science and a sanctuary for magic and myth. In many spiritual traditions, to go as far as the forest is to relinquish illusions and come in contact with ultimate reality. The priestly class of ancient Celts called Druids, the "seers of oaks," sought mystical

10

truth in groves of trees. The ancient Greeks came to the forest in their Dionysian rites, seeking an ecstatic union with the primeval forces of life and death. The Buddha left behind his privileged and pampered existence as a prince and went to the forest to live as a poor hermit, finding enlightenment as he sat meditating under the bodhi tree. In folktales and fairy tales, myths and legends, sacred stories and tales of adventure, we go as far as the forest to lose ourselves and then discover who we really are. We come to be transformed.

Some years ago, John Cook's great-great-grandson Anthony E. Cook published a book of gorgeous color photographs he called *The Cook Forest: An Island in Time*. For someone who has never been here, the book captures some of the forest's artistry, at various times of the year, in all sorts of light. For those who can't spend years exploring the forest, as he has, it captures images of some of the wild diversity of life existing here along with the old trees: mushrooms, spiders, newts, ferns, deer, and great horned owls, pileated woodpeckers, blackburnian warblers, red squirrels, and black bears. Each of his photographs is a work of art. But no one photograph can ever take in the entirety of even one of the ancient trees. They are both too tall and too imposing, too unique and too thrilling to photograph, much less to describe.

The old-growth forest is indescribably beautiful, but it is not always the safest place to be. Here in Cook Forest, Dale Luthringer leads us to a glade where the ground is littered with pieces of blasted bark and wood—"shrapnel" from a pine tree literally blown to bits by lightning. "This is not where you want to be in a storm," Luthringer warns us. The shattered tree will be left as it is on the forest floor, destroyed not by the buzz of a chain saw but by the power unleashed in a thunderstorm, a power greater than any weapon we have thought to make. Nature is not always benign, but Native American people, I know, consider fragments of wood like this to be holy, touched by the gods of thunder and lightning. Leaving the glade, I try to picture the tempest, the tall trees swaying in a furious wind, the deafening roar of thunder shaking the ground, the searing flash of a lightning bolt tearing the tree apart. I know I might not have survived such a storm. Still, I think, I would like to have been there.

CHAPTER TWO

Urban Forest

❦

Bruce Kershner has a habit of ending his sentences with exclamation points. "Look at that!" he says, pointing to a photograph of six-hundred-year-old cedar trees clinging to the cliffs of the Niagara Gorge. "Unbelievable!"

Co-founder of the Western New York Old Growth Forest Survey and Vice President of the New York Old Growth Forest Association, Kershner has made a career out of finding the most impressive ("the largest! the oldest! the most valuable!") trees in New York State. He's found them in or near the places most people are least likely to look—our cities.

Most old-growth forest in New York State is found near cities, he tells the audience of several hundred people who have come to hear him speak in the heart of an urban environment, at Buffalo's Museum of Science, on a warm night in August. To prove his point, he shows slides of ancient oaks in a grove behind a school in North Syracuse, a four-hundred-year old tulip tree he found growing in Queens, and trees he calls "living skyscrapers" in the twenty-five acres of old-growth forest he discovered at Inwood Hill Park, on the northern tip of Manhattan Island. ("In Manhattan!" he exclaims. "I couldn't believe it!") One of the reasons for so much old growth in urban areas is that wealthy families such as the Rockefellers, who held land like Inwood Hill privately for generations, didn't need the income from logging and could afford to appreciate the forest's scenic value. Then they deeded the properties to the public for parks. Left alone for centuries, the trees in these small forests all over New York State have grown to what Kershner, in typical hyperbolic style, calls "mega flora." He says these are "the huggable trees," the ones with trunks so large your arms can't reach around them—but that shouldn't stop you from trying. The best way to gauge the true size of a very large tree, he writes in one of his guidebooks, is to walk right up to it and put your arms around the trunk. "Besides," he adds, "after centuries of enduring hurricanes and windstorms, lightning, disease, droughts and vandalism, wouldn't you want a hug, too?"

Kershner is on a campaign to end what he calls "institutional denial" of the old-growth status of such urban forests, many of which are endangered, and he has personally fought commercial developers, private land owners, and even New York State's Department of Conservation to prove, first, that such places exist, and second, that they deserve protection.

Practiced at making his case in front of an audience, he enumerates the reasons to value even the smallest old-growth forests. They harbor the country's oldest, largest, and tallest living things. They are "living laboratories" for studying a forest's natural processes. Old-growth forests are concentrated habitats for endangered species. They are "genetic banks" for the strongest and most valuable genes of a species—those that have produced the tallest and hardiest trees. They have commercial value for eco-tourism, with the capacity to improve local property values, more so than another outlet mall. They are precious examples of our historic heritage, places to glimpse what North America looked like prior to the arrival of European settlers.

Most important, perhaps, to Kershner, they provide the intangible quality of inspiration. "Inspiration is what I'm after," he says. He quotes the Roman philosopher Seneca: "If you ever come upon a grove of ancient trees which have grown to an exceptional height, shutting out a view of sky by a veil of thickly intertwined branches, then the loftiness of the forest, the stillness of the place and your marvel at the thick unspoken shade in the midst of the open spaces will prove to you the presence of deity."

As part of his campaign for public awareness of old-growth forests, Kershner has written nine guidebooks, including *Guide to Ancient Forests in Vicinity of New York City* and *Secret Places of Staten Island*. His most recent, *The Sierra Club Guide to the Ancient Forests of the Northeast*, co-authored with

Robert Leverett, describes 134 different sites where old-growth forests can be found in eight states: Pennsylvania, New York, Connecticut, Rhode Island, Massachusetts, Vermont, New Hampshire, and Maine. In the Hudson Valley and New York Metro area alone he lists twenty different properties. New York City's largest living creature, he writes, is a four-hundred-year-old tulip tree known as the Queens Giant, growing a mere two hundred feet from the Long Island Expressway. In the Bronx, Pelham Bay Park has a ten-acre forest of ancient tulip trees and oaks. The former Rockefeller estate at Inwood Hill Park, on the northern tip of Manhattan, has eleven different species of old-growth trees, including five different kinds of oak. The book gives detailed instructions for reaching each of these properties, instructions sometimes resembling those for an urban walking tour. City dwellers can reach Inwood Hill Park, for instance, on the subway: "Take the A train to 207th street station," he writes. "Walk west two blocks. Turn right on Seaman Avenue, go four blocks to its end, and turn left on 218th street. Enter the park here."

Kershner also leads tours to some of the forests he thinks deserve special attention, and a few days after his Science Museum lecture, I join one of his tours. A group of twenty people, including myself, fourteen other women, and five men, are going with Kershner to DeVeaux Woods State Park in Niagara Falls. Kershner grew up on Staten Island, so he is uniquely qualified to appreciate urban forests. He now lives outside of Buffalo, and he has spent years exploring the patchwork of old-growth forest remaining in western New York. People make the mistake, he says, of assuming that once European settlers arrived two hundred years ago, the ancient forests disappeared as a result of logging and agricultural clearing. It's true that eighty percent or more of the Northeast's forests were cut down, and most of what we see today is second growth. But Kershner maintains that approximately four hundred thousand acres of old growth remain in the region. They are often on small parcels—DeVeaux Woods, for instance, is a ten-acre grove. Many ecologists, he feels, overlook forests that are not in large wilderness areas, or those which are not pristine and undisturbed. Such forests are not what we think of as "virgin," meaning original, untouched, and undisturbed. But "old growth," Kershner says,

15

refers to age. "If most of the canopy trees in a forest are ancient," he says, meaning a hundred fifty years or older, "—regardless of minor disturbance or size of stand—then the grove is ancient."

Ancient is the word for the Niagara River Gorge. It was formed twelve thousand years ago, at the end of the last ice age, when the ice retreated and the Niagara River began to flow over a large cliff, forming the famous falls. For thousands of years, falling water carved through the shale of the Niagara Escarpment, gradually receding southward as it eroded the cliff, leaving a gorge seven miles long in its wake. Along the escarpment, high over the gorge, a mighty oak forest grew. DeVeaux Woods is all that remains of that forest. From lookouts on the Niagara Gorge trails, using binoculars, cedars as old as six hundred years or more can be seen still growing on the cliffs of the gorge. But we don't need binoculars to see the oak trees in DeVeaux Woods State Park. We can walk right up to them.

Like many of the urban forests Kershner has discovered, DeVeaux Woods was once owned by a wealthy man, Judge Samuel DeVeaux, an early citizen of Niagara Falls. In 1853, he deeded the property to the DeVeaux College for Orphans and Destitute Children. The college later became a military prep school, and in 1978 it was purchased by Niagara University. Nine buildings are left on the property, including two from the mid-nineteenth-century era of the college for orphans. The Castellani Art Gallery was built here in 1978 to house grocery-store mogul Armand Castellani's art collection, which has moved, along with the university, to a new site a few miles up the road.

What we are here to see, however, are the ten acres of hardwood forest on the property, where oak trees dating back to the mid 1700s still grow. P. M. Eckel, a botanist with the Buffalo Museum of Science, wrote in her 1986 study of the area: "DeVeaux College woods is the oldest, most unaltered woodland along the entire American Gorge, including the Falls area." Yet in 1993, Niagara University decided to sell the property to developers who planned to build condominiums here. This stretch of land lies directly opposite one of the most attractive neighborhoods in Niagara Falls, prime real estate where expensive homes line the Lewiston Road. Environmentalists, including Kershner himself, persuaded the university to reconsider the sale in order to save the forest, and eventually, the property was purchased instead by the state of New York.

But the "incredible recreational educational opportunity" of De Veaux Woods, as Governor George Pataki termed it when he announced in May 2000 that the DeVeaux College property would become New York's 159th state park, is still a work in progress. Baseball diamonds and open fields on the southern end of the property closest to the highway are used, as they have been for years, by the Little League and the Boy Scouts, and rest rooms have been built near the ball fields. But an education-oriented nature center is only in the planning stages. An enormous pile of mulch has been dumped next to the DeVeaux College's utility building, and weeds have grown up around it. Inside the long, one-story building that is the old Castellani Art Gallery, offices, classrooms, and exhibition spaces are gathering dust. There are buildings ready and waiting to be converted into a nature center, and there is even ample parking for visitors. But so far, the De Veaux Woods Nature Center is only a dream.

As our group walks past the utility building to find the trail into the woods, we know we are in an urban forest by the sound of traffic reaching us from nearby roads. The ten acres of forest are sandwiched between Route 104 (Lewiston Road) on the east, and the Robert Moses Parkway on the west. We can also hear the rotary blades of the helicopters beating the air over the Niagara Gorge. But as we follow the trail into the woods, we're seeing the last remnants of the great oak forests that lined the Niagara River in pre-European-settlement times. "This is one of the finest oak forests in all of upstate New York!" Kershner announces. "This is just an amazing place!"

The tall trees here rise a hundred feet and more above us, their leafy canopy blocking out much of the sun. Kershner says that this woods has ancient black oak, red oak, white oak, and some sugar maples. Leathery brown oak leaves form a layer of mulch on the ground, which is also littered with small, fallen branches from the straight, tall trees. One of the signs of an old-growth forest, Kershner says, is trees that have lost most of their lower limbs as they reach towards the light for a hundred years or more. The crowns of these trees are so high that we can't distinguish the shapes of the leaves we see above us. Under the trees, moss covers the boulders I see here and there. It has been a summer of nearly constant rain in western New York, resulting in one of the top ten summer rainfalls on record here, and a typically heavy rain fell most of the previous night. Mosquitoes are out in force, and cans of insect-repellent spray come out of backpacks. I pull on a jacket for protection. Out on the ball fields, a jacket would have been uncomfortable on such a warm and humid day. But under the oak trees, the temperature seems as much as ten degrees cooler. In the shade of the tree canopy little else grows, and the light is muted, as if humbled. In comparison to the trees, our group of human beings feels tiny, insignificant, and very young, although the average age probably approaches sixty.

As we walk into the woods, I notice a round piece of broken glass—what looks like the bottom of a beer bottle—and kick it off the trail. Today the woods also show evidence of destruction by those who recognize the commercial value of a two-hundred-year-old oak tree in modern times. We are only a short distance into the woods when Kershner leads us off the trail to look at the enormous, ragged stump of a red oak, crowned by a wedge of its own wood, the same wedge chopped from its trunk to fell it.

"This is very interesting," Kershner says, as if thinking out loud. "I'm not sure why it would be cut. Why would it be cut if it's not endangering anybody?"

"Maybe it was leaning," someone says.

"Maybe the tree was going to fall," adds someone else.

"Fall on what?" Kershner asks.

"On us!" says a woman in the group.

"But there's no hazard," Kershner says. "Nobody walks through here. The trail's over there." He points to where we have been walking.

"Maybe it was cut a long time ago, before it was protected land," someone says.

"This is not that long ago—it has all of its bark and everything," says Kershner. "It's not rotted. This is within five years."

"Somebody did the wrong thing," another woman in the group says.

"It's very odd," Kershner says, his eyebrows raised in suspicion. With his thinning dark hair and inquisitive manner, he reminds me of a Lt. Columbo without the rumpled raincoat. Instead, he wears rumpled hiking pants tucked into his boots, and a blue T-shirt with a silk-screened image of a wolf perched on a rocky ledge, howling at the moon. "Anyway," he says, "let's find out how old it is." Slipping off his glasses and leaning in to peer at what's left of the tree, he begins to count its annual rings, and reaches 133 rings in ten inches of trunk. Looking at the size of the tree's hollow trunk, and estimating four more inches, he extrapolates that another fifty years of growth would be represented there, for a total of approximately 185 years.

"There's something strange going on here," Kershner says, putting on his glasses and standing back to look at the stump. "There was no reason for them to take it out." Local citizens who care about the woods, Kershner tells us, report that "things are happening" here. There is evidence that people are cutting trees and hauling off wood from the forest. The tracks of wheelbarrows have been found, tracks going out of the woods and disappearing between some of the nearby houses—houses so near that we can catch glimpses of them between the trees. Park police have found the wood of cut trees in people's yards. Without actual videotapes or an eyewitness to illegal cutting, however, it's impossible to prove that the wood came from this tree or one of the others in DeVeaux Woods. So far no one has been prosecuted. But as in any urban environment, constant vigilance is required to warn vandals away from valuable property—in this case, very old, very rare, and very valuable hard wood. The wood from a tree like this could have easily been worth thousands of dollars.

Kershner says the fact that this tree was hollow inside is not unusual. "Old-growth trees are often found to be hollow and it doesn't indicate illness," he says. "It doesn't even indicate weakness. It's very odd, but about fifty percent of the time when old-growth trees become hollow they become stronger structurally. There's a law of physics that when you have an inner surface and an outer surface you're stronger than when you're just solid." Trees like California's giant sequoias can live for thousands of years with hollow trunks, he says. When they fall, it's not because the wood breaks; they get ripped out of the ground, toppled by wind or the weight of ice on their limbs.

"Now recognize that this is a small oak," Kershner says. "We'll see oaks that are much, much bigger. This is small."

We walk back to the trail and come across a tall red oak; Kershner points out its old-growth features. "This is unusual for an oak," he says, as we gather around to study it. "You notice the swollen trunk base here?" he says. The tree's trunk has spread out at its base, looking as if it is stretching big moss- and lichen-covered toes into the ground. This "buttressing" or swollen base occurs, Kershner says, when the trunk of the tree has grown so tall that it is buffeted by wind, and must brace itself nearer the ground to avoid being toppled. Only an old-growth tree will have this kind of base, its tree wisdom allowing it to live a hundred and fifty years or more.

Kershner then points to the tree's shaggy gray bark, another sign of a very old tree. Stretching and straining with the tree as it grew for hundreds of years, the bark has begun to pull away from the wood in shaggy strips that you can almost put your hand under. "This is unusual for an oak," Kershner says again. "When you see bark like this, whether it's on a street tree or a forest tree, it has to be old growth." He estimates this tree to be approximately 175 years old.

"Let's move on," he says. He sets a brisk pace along the trail and our group tries to keep up with him as he strides through the forest, talking as he goes and brandishing a carved wooden walking stick. "This is what Niagara Falls and all of Niagara County looked like 250 years ago," he says over his shoulder. "Try to imagine that! And the towering trees! My god!"

20   Once we are deeper into the woods he leads us off the trail again to another oak tree. "This is the largest one in the woods," he says. "This tree is probably in the area of 315 years old is my guess. A magnificent specimen of red oak. Notice that its lowest bough is about thirty-five feet up." We tilt our heads back, trying to gauge the distance. "It means that the tree was always in the shade. It might have taken a hundred years to get that tall. Why? Because it had to aim straight up at the

light." The presence of so many trees with soaring branchless trunks is one indication that this forest has been a living entity for hundreds of years—all that time, the younger trees have been reaching for light above the canopy of the older, taller trees. This particular tree might have been growing here since 1689, when Niagara Falls was little more than a whispered legend, a wondrous place of thundering waters so mesmerizing that it was said a man might lose his senses if he gazed at the monstrous cascade too long.

A woman in the group asks about the difference between red oak and white oak, and Kershner explains the differences in the color and texture of the bark, along with the different shapes of their leaves. The bark of white oak is paler than that of other oaks, and has straighter scoring. Red oak leaves have pointed lobes, and white oak's are rounded off. He adds that the red oak takes its name from the brilliant red color of its leaves in fall. The same woman asks if there are many white oak to be seen here. "If you were the most valuable tree in the forest, would there be many of you?" Kershner responds. "White oak is the most stolen tree. But we'll see some."

We find an old sugar maple first, which Kershner estimates is well over two hundred years old. Tolerant of shade, the sugar maple has grown here among the oak trees, and high above us, one side of it has taken the clawed shape of a "staghorn" top, a form indicative of great age, caused by centuries of damage from ice and wind breaking off the ends of branches, which then sprout upwards. The sugar maple also has extremely shaggy bark. "That is a shaggy, shaggy, sugar maple," Kershner says, standing back to look at the tree. "When you see a sugar maple like that along a country road, even if it's planted, you'll know it was planted 150 years ago."

We continue walking, and a few minutes later he points to a tree with a different kind of bark. "This is a white oak, here. Notice the white bark. But it's balding. It's an old, old tree. It's all weathered, that's what it is." The weathering of the grayish-white bark into smooth, bare patches is another sign of a tree that has lived for over a hundred years. Trees that display bald patches, shaggy bark, deeply grooved bark, or platy bark are all signs of venerable age. It's surprising that this tree has survived so long, considering the value of its wood. Strong and rot resistant, white oak lumber brings top dollar because of its value for home building, especially flooring, as well as for fine cabinetry. Even the wine industry values the wood of white oak for making long-lasting, waterproof staves for barrels to hold vintage wine.

Further into the woods, we come across the gray, bare trunk of a tree that has died. "Here we have what's called a snag, which is simply a standing dead tree," Kershner says, "and for a long time foresters were told to get rid of these. Now we know that they're apartment houses for all kinds of wild life—owls, woodpeckers. Some of these snags remain standing for a long period of time. And they're also nesting sites for hawks and owls and eagles." He tells us that in the Zoar Valley, site of an old-growth forest in Cattaraugus County, the first nesting bald eagles found since the 1970s have been spotted. "Guess why?" Kershner asks, and then answers his own question. "Old-growth snags."

We circle back through the forest, passing the jagged trunk of the red oak chopped down so recently, and soon we are glimpsing the DeVeaux College buildings once more. "Now you're getting sensitized to the way of seeing antiquity on a tree," Kershner says as we step out into the parking lot once more. "You may see street trees, yard trees, field trees, or forest trees, and you'll know they're old."

❧

Back in Wellsville the next evening, I go out to look at the trees in my own neighborhood. Tall trees line our street, and their stately beauty was one of the features that first attracted me here. It's an old neighborhood; our house, built in 1971, is the newest one on the block. Some of the homes are large and grand, some small and modest. Retired people live here alongside families with young children who walk back and forth to the school at the end of the street. Several houses date from the mid-nineteenth century, and on the corner of Brooklyn and West State Street is the famous "Pink House," a sprawling Victorian. Always painted pink, it is a local landmark, privately owned and reportedly haunted by the spirit of a young girl who drowned years ago in a small pond behind the house. Unlike houses built on the other side of town, many of the houses here are built on large lots, with space for back yards full of towering pine, oak, willow, maple, and ash. Right out near the sidewalks are some of the oldest specimens, dwarfing the houses they shade in summer time. Along with the many older homes, the old trees give this street a character conveyed only by longevity. The trees are also frequented by birds, like the sleek black ravens who glide back and forth overhead, surveying the street and croaking a constant reconnaissance in a kind of avian neighborhood watch and now and then leaving one of their beautiful, long black feathers for me to find in the yard. There are so many trees in this neighborhood that I often feel I am living in the midst of a small urban forest.

The words "urban" and "forest" may seem mutually exclusive, but to those concerned with the ecology of cities, the truth is that planting trees in cities and towns is an important way to reduce energy costs, combat pollution, and improve our quality of life. Urban trees shade buildings and help to cool them in summer, reducing the cost of air conditioning. According to the University of Washington's Center for Urban Horticulture, a well-established urban tree canopy can reduce summer air temperatures by as much as ten degrees. Trees protect us from ultra-violet rays and filter carbon dioxide emissions from the air, reducing smog. By collecting rainwater and diverting it to their roots, trees function as low-cost storm-drainage systems.

Trees can even be crime fighters. Urban housing projects lacking flowers and trees report nearly twice as many crimes as those that are landscaped. Research on housing projects, prisons, and nursing homes shows that anxiety and aggression increase among people who consistently lack a view of natural things. And trees can heal. Research by environmental psychologist Robert Ulrich has demonstrated that patients with a view of trees outside their windows require less pain medication, report less anxiety, and have fewer post-operative complications than patients whose hospital windows look out on treeless parking lots.

The oldest trees in a neighborhood also help us to maintain a connection with the past. But tall, old street trees make homeowners and power companies nervous. If the trees fall in windstorms or ice storms, they can cause damage to property and power lines. Losing their older branches here and there, they begin to lose their decorative appeal. So a few years ago, our public works department cut down many

23

of the less attractive older trees on the strip of grass between sidewalk and street considered village property. No one had been notified. We just came home from work one day and found the trees reduced to stumps. A few days later, the stumps were dug up and ground into dust. Some, like the two old maples in front of our house, growing close to a major power line supplying the neighborhood with electricity, were not replaced. The trees taken from further down the street were replaced with young specimens of Norway maple, a popular street tree known for what horticulturists call "plasticity." Norway maple is easily manipulated to produce cultivars with strikingly colored foliage, from the bright green of "Emerald Jade" to the dark cabernet red of the one called "Crimson King."

This process of cutting trees and replanting them has gone on several times in the history of the neighborhood. I can see that in the different ages and types of trees planted along the street. Many of the newcomers are the non-native Norway maple variety, and despite their reputation for hardiness, they don't look healthy. It is only the end of August, but already some of them are beginning to lose their leaves. I pick up a fallen maple leaf and see the telltale signs of tar spot disease, raised black spots that look just like the leaf has been splattered with tar. It's not tar, but an outbreak of fungus, caused by two extremely wet springs. When the fungus gets into the leaf petioles that attach leaves to the tree's branches, it causes the leaves to drop prematurely. Norway maples have long been popular for street planting in cities and towns across the northern United States because they are easy to obtain and they grow quickly. But the truth is that non-native varieties of trees like the Norway maple can also be vulnerable to diseases that native trees learned long ago to survive.

A hundred years ago, our village favored a different kind of tree, one native to our own continent—the sugar maple. A few of these old giants remain, some on lawns close to the sidewalk, and some on the strip between sidewalk and street. They are the neighborhood's oldest residents, and despite their age, they often look healthier than the newcomers. Their leaves are green and free of tar-spot. But it is not only their vigor that makes them an inspiration. More than any other form, it is the sugar maple, with its tall, branching shape and its autumn crown of crimson and gold that defines the character of old village streets like this one. Tolerant of human society's sidewalks, pipes, and drains, equally indifferent to summer's blistering heat or winter's freezing cold, and with an almost classical grace in the strong, spreading form of their branches, sugar maples were once the tree of choice in towns and villages all over the northeastern United States. As much as the architecture of the Victorian age, they define the way an old New England town should look in our imagination. But they have become so valuable, both for their "heritage" status and their wood—not to mention the sweet sap they make in spring—that they are far more pricey these days than they once were. Too pricey, perhaps, for some communities.

Or perhaps people are simply seduced by the new and different, lured by the exotic stranger who seems to promise something better than the past.

Still, while other trees have come and gone in this neighborhood, a few of the old sugar maples endure. The one growing outside the white clapboard house at 230 West State Street appears to be the oldest. Fifty feet tall, it clears the power lines easily. I take Bruce Kershner's advice, walk right up to it and try to put my arms around its trunk. I'm surprised to find that it takes two of my arm spreads to reach around the trunk—it's a full twelve feet around. Its bark is another country, full of ridges and gorges, moss-covered peaks and valleys of lichen the color of copper verdigris, giving the bark its scaly patina of age. The tree has also stretched massive, buttressed toes towards the hand-carved slate stones of the street's original sidewalk—the stones have raised a bit around it, but they've held. Some ten feet up, the tree splits into two branches. Thirty feet higher, it fills the sky with its five-lobed, pointed leaves, a galaxy of green stars.

This tree looks nearly as old as the sugar maple we saw in DeVeaux Woods, perhaps a hundred and fifty years. Since it was planted, generations of children have played here, grown up, and gone. Rain has washed the colored chalk of their hopscotch games away, for now, but next summer another group of children will come out to play on the sidewalk under the tree. Winter, spring, and fall, they will walk from here to the school at the end of the street and back again under the branches of the ancient tree. All the while the lichen will grow on the bark of the sugar maple towering over the street. And on cloudless nights like this one, the crescent moon must first clear the line of trees to be seen, a sliver of silver in the sky.

CHAPTER THREE
Sweet Dreams

When the barren trees on the hillside stretch shadows like long blue fingers across the snow, and the snow retreats to patches of crusty white foam on the forest floor

when the days grow nearly as long as the nights, and the twin stars Castor and Pollux in the constellation of Gemini are nearly overhead,

when the northern hemisphere turns its face to the sun and the sky turns opalescent with the approach of spring,

then the sweet sap of the maple trees rises from the roots where it has waited all winter underground, and the time for sugaring has come.

As with all hardwood trees that live in cold climates, dormancy is the maple tree's adaptation to winter. Birds fly south, bears succumb to the twilight sleep of hibernation, foxes and squirrels grow luxurious coats of fur to survive the season. Hardwood trees simply drop their leaves, send their sap underground, and stand silently waiting for spring. They have already set the buds that will become new leaves, ready to open when spring's sunlight warms them. Sleeping under the stars, a tree in the northern forest marks time not in hours or moments, as Bernd Heinrich points out in his book *The Trees in My Forest*, but in seasons. And just as winter turns to spring, in the dream time after the sap begins to rise and before the tender new leaves unfurl, for a few short weeks the sweet sap of the sugar maple tree can be harvested to make one of North America's unique and most popular products: maple syrup.

Native to this part of the world, the sugar maple can live up to four hundred years, and with its spreading, broad crown of leaves, it collects sunlight to make the sugars that sweeten its sap. Trees growing in open

27

fields or along a street, like the ancient sugar maples on my own street in Wellsville, will have sweeter sap than those in a forest, or even in a commercial sugar bush where the trees are grown for tapping, because their crowns have more room to spread out and produce more leaves than forest trees growing close together and competing for space and light. Sap with a higher sugar content requires less evaporation time to boil down to syrup, and a bigger tree can take more taps. On a good day of sap flow, each tap might produce a gallon of sap. I wonder if the sugar maples here in the village of Wellsville ever held buckets to collect their sap. If they did, the tap holes have long ago healed over. Tapping does not permanently harm a tree, as long as it is done in spring, when the tree has energy and the long season of growth ahead to heal.

The actual sugar content of a sugar maple's sap varies from one to three percent; in rare instances, it can be as high as ten percent. Boiled until most of the water has evaporated, the sap thickens into syrup with a concentration of sixty to seventy percent sugar, making it recognizably sweet, along with the delectable flavor we have come to know as "maple." Maple syrup expert Mariafranca Morselli, a biochemist at the University of Vermont, says the chemical elements of pure maple syrup are so complex that they can't be duplicated in the laboratory. They come from the day-to-day travels of the sap as it acquires its souvenirs of sucrose, amino acids, tannins, and minerals—including calcium, potassium, and iron—from the tree and the soil where the tree is growing. Morselli is only one of many scientists studying the mysteries of the sugar maple. All maples have sweet sap; why is the sap of the aptly named sugar maple the sweetest? Even the scientists aren't sure. Cornell University conducts research on maple trees at their center near Lake Placid, New York, producing "sweet tree" saplings the scientists hope will have good growth rates, better sap yield, and higher sugar content. At the New York State Agricultural Experiment Station in Geneva, maple specialists are investigating how the sweet sap of the maple can be used for making new products like maple jelly, maple mustard, and maple peanuts. But the sugar makers themselves are sometimes the best innovators. At Flyway Farms in Medina, New York, Pat Laubisch has created a maple seasoning to use

28

on grilled meats, French-fried potatoes, and scrambled eggs. It's made of herbs, salt, pepper, garlic, and the granulated maple sugar she and her husband Terry make from the sap of maple trees on their farm. At Sprague Maple Farms in Portville, Randy Sprague makes maple sausage to serve at the restaurant he built on his farm in the year 2000, marking the start of a new millennium for maple syrup.

Exactly how and when people first discovered the potential hidden in the "sweet water" that comes from maple trees at this time of year is unknown, but most historians credit North America Indians with passing on their knowledge to European settlers. With an intimate knowledge of the forest, Native Americans found a use for every part of the tree. Bark was dried, pounded, powdered, and boiled to make dyes. Sticky sap and leaves made poultices for wounds; twigs, leaves, roots, and bark steeped in hot water made medicinal teas. Each tree had different properties, and different uses; indigenous people studied them all. So it is not surprising that Native Americans discovered the secret to making maple sugar. Their oral traditions are rich with sugaring stories, legends and tales of a man or a woman who first guessed that the sap oozing from a maple tree in early spring could be boiled down to make the sweet, sustaining sugar we all crave. My favorite is an Iroquois tale relating how a woman noticed the sap dripping from the bark of a tree where her husband had left his tomahawk. Collecting the sap and adding it to her stew, she found it sweetened when it had been heated. I like the way this story gives a woman credit for the discovery, and knowing how men can be careless about where they put their tools, I think it has the ring of truth.

By the mid 1500s French explorers traveling to Canada learned of the maple trees and their sweet sap from the Indians there. By the 1600s, the British were reporting that the indigenous people of Canada made "incisions" in the maple tree, let the sap run, collected it in bark vessels, and used hot rocks to boil it down to sugar. Molten sap was ready to cool into sugar if it formed a golden taffy when drizzled on the snow. ("Sugar on snow" is still an old-fashioned ritual for anyone who makes their own maple syrup; you can imitate the process by heating some pure maple syrup on the stove and serving it atop bowls heaped with freshly fallen snow—or failing that, vanilla ice cream freshly gathered from the freezer.) Native Americans used maple sugar to flavor game, and consumed it as a staple when game was scarce. After the "snow moon" of February had passed, the name given to the full moon of March was the "sugar moon."

Winter-weary European settlers soon learned to mimic the native methods, substituting big iron kettles for birch bark trays. In the northeastern forest, maple sugar was free for the taking, unlike the expensive cane sugar imported from warmer climes, and sugaring time came conveniently when other farm chores were minimal, between autumn harvesting and spring planting. Sugaring also provided some extra income in winter. Thomas Jefferson, on a visit to Vermont in 1791, was so intrigued with the maple's potential as a cash crop that he ordered sixty maple saplings to plant at Monticello and urged George Washington to do the same at Mount Vernon. "I have never seen a reason why every farmer should not have a sugar orchard as well as an apple orchard," he wrote. "The supply of sugar for his family would require as little ground, and the process of making it as easy as that of cider." Virginia turned out to be too warm for sugaring. Still, in the nineteenth century, abolitionists promoted maple sugar as a replacement for sugar cane that was harvested as a result of the blood and tears of slaves in the West Indies.

In the nineteenth century, sugar making also became an industry. With the introduction of tin to make taps, collecting buckets, cans for preserving the liquid syrup, and the all-important evaporating pans for boiling large quantities of sap, maple syrup could be made in quantity and shipped around the world just as it is today. But even with today's hi-tech collection systems and oil-powered evaporators, I find it hard to imagine a more labor-intensive process. Some forty gallons of sap must be boiled to make one gallon of pure maple syrup, which is nowadays considered a luxury item, selling for between thirty and forty dollars. It's no wonder that modern maple syrup producers still strive to evoke the romantic age of horse-drawn wagons, tin collecting buckets, and the sweet steam wafting from the chimney of the old-fashioned sugar shack in the woods in order to convince consumers to spend so much for the real thing, when imitation maple syrup at the supermarket costs a fraction as much.

But the connoisseur hardly needs convincing. Tasting the smooth, liquid amber of pure maple syrup soaking into homemade griddle cakes is like tasting the forest. John Burroughs called it "a wild delicacy of flavor" and "the distilled essence of the tree." Since moving to western New York, where every other country road has a hand-lettered sign somewhere along the way reading "Maple Syrup for Sale," I've become a pure maple syrup snob. New York ranks right behind Vermont in maple syrup production, and within a few miles from my home, I can choose syrup for sale from a half dozen different makers. Like vineyards, I think, each sugar bush of maple trees has its own *terroir*, a character derived from the unique combination of soil, water, light, and altitude at its location. Like vintage wine, I think, each year's product is different, and each year, sugar makers anxiously watch and wait for the right combination of cold nights and warm days to tell them it's time for the sap to run. It's all a matter of timing. Without temperatures below freezing overnight and at least a fifteen degree "swing" to higher temperatures during the day, the sweet sap will not flow. Once the tree's leaves begin to come out, the sap loses its flavor. Depending on conditions, the season can last as long as six weeks, or as briefly as ten days, stopping and starting as the temperature changes. The length of the sap run will make or break a sugar producer's year.

In New York, 2004 was a difficult year for a variety of reasons. A cold, damp summer in 2003 meant sunlight was scarce and the sugar content of the maple sap was lower than usual. That meant more gallons of sap had to be boiled to produce one gallon of syrup. To make matters worse, deep snows across the state as the season began kept sugar makers out of the woods several weeks longer than usual. The taps must be drilled freshly each season, and sugar makers here like to start opening taps sometime late in February. Some had to get to their trees on snowshoes. Despite all the obstacles, the 2004 harvest in New York State yielded some 255,000 gallons of pure maple syrup, nearly a fifth of the country's total production. Producers in the state's southern tier fared better than those in the north, where windstorms damaged trees and tap lines.

Once, there was the plinking sound of sap dripping into hundreds of tin buckets hung under the taps to collect the maple trees' sap. Now, when I walk the ridge tops surrounding Wellsville, I often see the blue plastic tap lines strung from one tree to another in someone's sugar bush. No more spring plinking; the gravity-fed lines silently move hundreds of gallons of sap to collecting tanks in the woods much more efficiently than the laborious lifting and carrying of sap-filled buckets. But wander through an old stand of sugar maple here, and you're still apt to find artifacts of the nineteenth century—a discarded wooden bucket, a pile of stones built up against a tree where the bucket was set to catch some sap dripping from the spile, a tube driven into the hole drilled into the tree. And almost everyone I know living in the countryside around Wellsville has tapped their trees at least once to make a little syrup. Some people eke out a sweet cup or two from one of their trees and drink the syrup as a kind of spring tonic, a promise of summer days to come.

I don't know if Pablo Neruda ever tasted maple syrup. Possibly not; he lived in Chile, in Cuba, in Italy, and in France, but none of these places are maple syrup country. He knew about honey, and in his poem "Dulce siempre," meaning "Sweetness, always," he recalls seeing a fantastic pyramid of colored sugar displayed in a confectionary shop window in the far off city of Madras, India. Neruda may not have known about maple syrup. But he certainly knew about sweetness. He understood that we crave sweetness not just as a pleasant taste, but as a need for something that transcends sustenance. He likened the longing for sweetness to sexual desire, "the love-needs of our bodies." The elemental need for something sweet is a guilty pleasure we don't like to admit to, but one he thought pointless to deny. "Don't be afraid of sweetness," he wrote.

> *With us or without us,*
> *Sweetness will go on living*
> *And is infinitely alive,*
> *Forever being revived,*
> *For it's in a man's mouth,*
> *Whether he's eating or singing,*
> *That sweetness has its place.*

Planting a tree requires a belief in the future. A native tree like the sugar maple grows slowly and lives long. But this means that the sugar maple sapling you plant today may not be ready to tap for another thirty years. Competing with each other for space and light, trees growing in the forest can take as long as fifty years to be ready to tap. As we walk up the hillside behind Sprague's Maple Farms Pancake House and Restaurant on a warm day in early February, Randy Sprague shows me maple trees that have been growing here for a hundred and fifty years. Despite extensive logging, old trees are not entirely unknown here, and I'm aware that pockets of old-growth hemlock, pine, and oak survive in the hills surrounding the farm. The maples here may have grown up some time after the loggers left in the mid 1800s, and they are very different in character from the sugar maples growing on my street back home. These are forest trees. Their trunks are straight and tall from many years of reaching for the sun, bare of branches for twenty-five feet or more. They have grown up rather than out, because their crowns had little room to spread. Their bark is shaggy, balding in places, mottled with moss and lichen in shades of verdigris, the patina of venerable old age.

Like so many sugar bushes in western New York, this hillside was once grazed by cattle on a dairy farm. Sprague purchased the property in 1992 and followed his childhood dream of becoming a sugar maker. He grew up a few blocks from here on Maple Street, so his life story, it seems, was written long ago. When I ask him how he got hooked on making maple syrup, his blue eyes shine, and he says "The smell. I always enjoyed the smell of the fresh syrup, the joy of being in the woods, the crispness of the air at early spring." He recalls seeing horse-drawn carts taken into the woods around Portville to collect the buckets of sap hanging from the trees, and as a boy he started out making his own syrup with just a few buckets he "rented" on the Van Deschler farm, the same property he now owns. Now, he has fifteen thousand taps going on several different properties, and he makes between one thousand and four thousand gallons of maple syrup every year, depending on the sap run. "The weather has to be just right," he says, with nighttime temperatures in the twenties and days in the forties. "The worst kind of weather is when it gets warm and stays warm." The

33

woody tissue in the trees is like a sponge, he explains. At night, when the temperature drops below freezing, the sponge absorbs the freezing sap. When the wood expands with warmer temperatures during the day, the sponge releases the sap.

Here on the rocky hillside, the old maple trees stand serenely among a few eastern hemlock, and the ground is slick with melting snow. A soft blue light drops over the hills as the sun dips towards the horizon. "We're not seeing a lot of regeneration here," Sprague says, eyeing the trees as we walk up the trail. Years of cattle grazing on the hillside damaged the forest in the past; now the problem is deer grazing. "It turns out that sugar maple saplings are one of the deer's favorite foods," Sprague says. The trunks of experimental saplings he is growing on a plot at the base of the hill are protected from the deer by tubular shields called tree guards; sugar makers are happy, he says, whenever the government supports thinning the deer herd across the state.

Growing in its native range, the sugar maple is an amazingly resilient and healthy tree, but sugar makers worry, and wonder if it will remain so in the new millennium. Could the sugar maple be wiped out by an infestation of insects or a catastrophic disease, as the American chestnut and the elm were? Everyone had a scare in 1982, when two large sugar bushes in Quebec suddenly died off. After years of study, the official explanation by the North American Maple Project is that the trees were killed by cold—two consecutive winters of severe cold without adequate snow cover to insulate the maples' roots. But like all the trees in our forests, sugar maples are suffering from acid rain, road salt, and climate change. Trees under multiple sources of stress are in particular danger. A few bad winters combined with too much acid rain combined with a plague of gypsy moths or another invasive pest like pear thrips could provide the tipping point. And if the climate of North America eventually warms to the point that sugaring season no longer exists, maple syrup as we know it now may also be just a memory.

⚜

This year, the first few weeks of March are frigid. Cold nights are followed by equally cold days; the temperature never gets above freezing. On the morning of March 19th, the vernal equinox is only a day away, and the weather is finally turning along with the season. The snow in our yard retreats, leaving bare patches of ground at the base of the trees. Standing by the window, I study the sky, its soft blue effulgence traced from south to north by the long, narrow V of a flock of geese flying high above me and heading for the river.

One of our resident ravens floats purposefully across the yard, a scrap of twig in its beak, and swoops into the branches of a tall Scotch pine in a row of three trees that grow close together, forming a dense and shadowy world of pine needles thirty feet high in the air. I see another bird, carrying another twig, coming in for a landing on the same spot on the tree. The pair busy themselves with their building a while, and then glide out again, their long black wings shiny as fresh ink in the morning sun. They have never nested this close to the house before, and I take it as a compliment. I also take it as an omen. Surely, the time for sugaring has come.

In fact, it is officially Maple Weekend in western New York, and I am going back to Sprague Maple Farms to visit the sugar house Randy Sprague has built on the south-facing hill of his sugar bush. The weather is perfect. The temperature was well below freezing overnight, and is expected to be in the forties by afternoon. Forty-one different maple producers in western New York are opening their sugar houses to the public, offering demonstrations and tastings along with the obligatory pancake breakfasts. The restaurant Randy Sprague built five years ago is a sprawling twenty-first-century interpretation of the traditional rustic huts with a few tables and benches where farm wives served griddle cakes dripping with syrup during sugaring season. His 13,000-square-foot building holds an evaporating plant, a filtering press, and rooms for bottling Sprague maple syrup, along with storerooms for tap lines and tools. The dining room has a cathedral ceiling, a fireplace, and huge, antler-horn-shaped chandeliers. The restaurant is open all year round, serving Friday night fish fries and Saturday night prime rib along with everyday roast turkey, maple baked beans, and maple milk shakes. You can still get pancakes at all times of the day and all times of the year, of course. The "L'il Tapper" special is two buttermilk pancakes with bacon or sausage. The "Big Run" is three pancakes, and the "Big Tapper," for those with a hearty appetite and no concerns about cholesterol, includes a six-ounce sirloin breakfast steak. "Sugar on snow" is a Belgian waffle topped with maple whipped cream and drizzled with maple syrup. Desserts include maple custard, maple pecan pie, and apple pie with maple cinnamon syrup. You can top it all off with a "Café Sugar House," a dessert coffee laced with Baileys and Kahlua, whipped cream, and of course, maple syrup. The restaurant's gift shop sells the Sprague brand syrups along with maple jelly, maple fudge, maple sugar, and at this time of year, the deliciously ephemeral maple cream, a pale, smooth spread made by heating the season's first syrup and then stirring it as it cools. Maple cream is difficult to make, forms mold easily, and consequently doesn't have much of a shelf life, so most people haven't tasted it, which is probably just as well. Having tried it, I have found it highly addictive.

I park in the lot outside the restaurant, and looking up the hill, I see a smear of white steam over the sugarhouse. Traditionally, when your neighbors saw the steam from your sugarhouse chimney, they would arrive to share both the labor and the harvest, and the forest became a social scene. Sugar making is hard work, and once the sap is collected, it has to be boiled within twenty-four hours, or it will spoil. It's a little after nine a.m. now, and Duncan Deschler has been at work for several hours already inside the sugarhouse, building the fire under the evaporator and boiling the sap in eight-foot-long stainless steel evaporating pans set over an old-fashioned cast-iron stove. The sap has just started to flow, he tells me, and yesterday was the first good "running day." If it rains tonight, as the weather forecast and the bones in my own neck and shoulders are telling me it will, the trees will be "weeping" sap tomorrow, Deschler says. "Rain makes it run hard, but only for so long," he claims. When warm temperatures prevail and the buds on the maple trees leaf out, the sap acquires a bitter taste that sugar makers call "buddy." Once this happens, the season is over. "You want to see a nice transition into spring, nice and slow," Deschler says, to make a good maple syrup season.

The wood he feeds into the fire is cut from the farm's own lots, and the fire makes the sugar house pleasantly warm. The clouds of steam coming off the boiling sap make it fragrant with the sweet dream of maple syrup, that intoxicating aroma that got Randy Sprague hooked on sugar making. It was Duncan Deschler's father Van, known affectionately in Portville as "Uncle Van," who taught Randy Sprague the art of sugar making, and eventually sold him this property. Duncan Deschler still lives across the road, and while he no longer farms, he still makes maple syrup here on the weekends at this time of year, as long as the season lasts. Using an evaporator much like this one, he and his father made between 130 and 140 gallons of syrup a year. Down at the base of the hill in the same building as the restaurant is a new, state-of-the-art reverse-osmosis evaporator Randy Sprague uses to make the much larger quantities of syrup he sells. The big evaporator down there runs at a temperature of nearly two thousand degrees Fahrenheit. But the wood fire here in the sugar house is plenty hot at six to seven hundred degrees. The new system is more energy-efficient and faster. But Sprague has created this replica of the old-fashioned sugar house to maintain a connection with the past, and Duncan Deschler helps to keep up the old traditions.

The new system of tubing that draws the sap from the trees on the hillside is not without maintenance problems, Deschler tells me. A crew of three men is out in the woods right now, checking the lines. Ice can break the lines and clog them; squirrels can chew on them. Bears, Deschler says, can make a good mess of a tap line, tearing it open to get at the sweet sap when they wake up, desperately hungry after a long winter's night of hibernation.

Unlike the quietly sterile operation of the hi-tech evaporator down at the restaurant, the old-fashioned sugar house is a multi-sensory experience. The wood fire under the evaporator sings; the syrup bubbles and boils. Standing over it, Duncan Deschler is half-obscured in clouds of sweetly fragrant steam. The rough-hewn hemlock beams of the sugar house are hung with artifacts of the past: old wooden sap buckets, antique sugar molds for making candy. When the sap is running hard, farmers have to be in their sugar houses day and night. Keeping the evaporating trays full of sap and keeping the fire stoked properly so that the sap continues to evaporate but doesn't boil over requires constant attention. On a day like today, at least, it wouldn't be unpleasant, and it isn't solitary work. Sooner or later, that sweetness draws a crowd.

At a little after ten o'clock, a tractor rumbles up the hill from the parking lot, dragging a large wooden cart full of people, followed by Randy Sprague in his gray Ford truck. With his wife Toni and two other women from the restaurant, he carries samples of Sprague syrup in large plastic pump containers, and Toni sets them up on the counter at the far side of the sugar house as the guests gather round the evaporator. "Boy, it sure smells good in here," says one of the men in the group. The children have had their faces painted with flowers and peace signs down at the restaurant, and they carry pink and white balloons. While the women make sugar on snow with syrup they've already filtered in the bottling plant at the restaurant and shaved ice in place of snow, I sample the three different grades of syrup in the plastic bottles, pumping them into little plastic cups. The dark grade, which is boiled the longest, is dark caramel-colored, thick and sweet. Some people favor this grade of syrup, but to me it doesn't taste as much of "maple" as it should. Perhaps the high sugar content obscures the more subtle flavor of the maple's sap. The medium-grade syrup is two or three shades lighter in color, less thick, and more recognizably maple. The grade labeled light is amber-colored, more watery, and it has what I think of as the true maple flavor, fresh and sharp as spring sunlight slanting through the tall old trees on the hill.

Watching the sap boil in the evaporator, at the other end of the room, Duncan Deschler samples it with a stainless-steel bailer, scooping up hot sap and pouring it out again to see how thick it is. The sap moves through three trays in the evaporator as it thickens, and a spigot on the last tray will release the syrup when it is ready. Eyeing the sap pouring off his bailer, Deschler says, "It's starting to wax," meaning it's getting close to becoming syrup. He starts pouring samples into a hydrometer to measure the hot sap's density. "It won't be too long," he says, tapping the gauge on the hydrometer with his index finger to judge the sap's resistance.

38

Another group of visitors arrive from the restaurant to crowd around the evaporator, and then, at ten thirty, after two hours of boiling the sap, Deschler opens the spigot on the side of the evaporator and releases the first hot syrup into a bucket. He closes the spigot, deftly lifts the full bucket on his shoulder, and carries it to a tub fitted with big paper filters. He pours in the syrup, covers the tub with a lid, and leaves the syrup to filter.

Taking a break from stoking the fire to step outside, Deschler shows me the lidded, galvanized-tin buckets hung on a number of the trees around the sugar house to demonstrate the old-fashioned way of collecting the sweet maple's sap. Pulling back one of the lids, he points to the sap that has accumulated in the bucket, about an inch or so. The spile is slowly dripping clear, clean sap. Once the sap really starts to run, the buckets will fill up quickly. Deschler says this south-facing hillside is ideal for tapping, because it warms up more quickly than the other side of the hill. He remembers that when he was a boy working on his father's farm he could barely get the morning chores done before finding buckets like these overflowing with sap. "It's amazing when they take off," he says.

The tin buckets give visitors like me a glimpse of what the sugar bush must have looked like fifty years ago, when the tall, straight trees all held buckets looking like bulging hip pockets. Most of the trees, however, are strung with narrow blue plastic tap lines feeding into larger white tubes carrying the sap to collecting tanks. I notice that among the tall old trees are skinny young saplings wearing the tubular white sheaths that protect them from deer. These trees come from the Cornell University program, not the forest. They will change the nature of the sugar bush, but Duncan Deschler says he approves. "You take care of the environment," he says, citing the farmer's creed. "What you take out, you put back in." He acknowledges that we won't know how it all turns out. "Randy won't see sap from these trees, but someone else will," Deschler says, meaning that the saplings growing here today won't be ready to tap for at least another thirty years.

Compared to other forests, the sugar bush has a well-mannered look. Paths have been made among the trees, and it's obvious that fallen and dying trees have been removed. The remaining old maples have an air of complacency conferred on them by age and nurtured by the respect and even the affection of those who come to tap their sweet sap in spring. Still, these are not plantation-bred trees. Long ago, they claimed the rocky, glacier-scraped soil of this hillside on their own initiative, and made this place their home.

Despite the cart full of people rumbling back down the hill to the restaurant and the gaggle of squealing children running past me down the path, pink and white balloons bobbing behind them, there is a calmness to the hour now as winter turns to spring. John Burroughs called it the season's equipoise, this time when the day is equal to the night.

I walk off the path to look at one of the oldest trees on the hillside. Snow still laps at its feet; moss and lichen decorate its deeply furrowed bark. A tin collecting bucket is hung on its side, and when I pull back the little peaked roof of the lid on the bucket, I can see that the sap is running. I slip my hand under the spile and catch a few drops of sap on my fingertips. Bringing my fingers to my mouth, I taste the tree's nectar—-soft and faintly sweet on my tongue. Water has come from the sky, and into the ground, up through the roots of the tree to its leaves, and back again, sweetened by sunlight. All winter the tree has stood dormant, dreaming of bringing this sweetness to my lips. Or was it I who dreamed of the tree?

CHAPTER FOUR
Appalachian Spring

❧

The Great Smoky Mountains are among the most storied places on earth. There is the story of mountains rising from an ancient sea two hundred million years ago, tectonic forces lifting layers of metamorphic rock to create the long range of peaks we call the Appalachians. There is the story of glaciers creeping southward from the pole during the last ice age, mile-high walls of ice that scraped away soil and drove off plants and animals, stopping just short of what is now Tennessee. Here was a refuge for the flora and fauna that eventually migrated northward to repopulate our forests when the glaciers finally withdrew.

There is the story of the Cherokee people, thought to be a breakaway group of the Iroquois, whose Eastern band made the Smokies their home a thousand years ago. They called the mountains *Schaconage*, meaning "the place of blue smoke," for the moist blue curtain of haze perpetually hanging on the hills. There is the story of the Scotch and Irish who arrived in the 1700s, fiercely hardy settlers who established small, self-sufficient communities in the fertile valleys of the Smokies, building cabins in the shadow of mist-shrouded mountains beside groves of giant trees. There is the cruel story of the Removal Act of 1830, which called for the relocation of all Indian people east of the Mississippi River, and the even crueler story of the Trail of Tears in 1838, when Andrew Jackson forced thirteen thousand of the Cherokee on a death march to Oklahoma. There is the story of the few thousand Cherokee who hid in the mountains and refused to leave, keeping to their way of life in isolated groups until they were granted a reservation in 1889.

There is the story of timber cutting, and the railroads that made possible large-scale logging that destroyed much of what had been primeval forests of hemlock, pine, spruce, fir, oak, maple, chestnut, and a hundred other different types of trees. Even the Cherokee cut and sold the timber on their land, desperate, like many who lived in the mountains, for a way to survive. Finally, in the twentieth century, there is the story of the $12.7 million raised from both private and public donors to purchase half a million acres of land to create Great Smoky Mountains National Park.

In the end, they are all one story, embodying one truth: a fight to survive. The forests of the Great Smoky Mountains, straddling the borders of Tennessee and North Carolina, are still some of the largest, the oldest, the most diverse, and the most beautiful on earth. They are also some of the most endangered.

"We're in a race against time," says forester Kristine Johnson when I meet with her in April. We are sitting in a basement office at Great Smoky Mountains National Park Headquarters, a few hundred feet from the Sugarlands Visitors' Center. With her long legs and her long, honey-colored hair, Johnson has the looks of a dancer, but like everyone else who works here, she is clad in National Park Service-issue khaki pants and shirt, and wears laced-up hiking boots on her feet. I have come here to ask her about the fight to save the hemlock trees in the park from an insect that has already destroyed hemlock forests over much of Appalachia. Called the hemlock woolly adelgid (*Adelges tsugae*) the tiny Asian insect first appeared in Oregon in the 1920s. It surfaced near Richmond, Virginia in the 1950s, and since then it has spread gradually east. In 2002, it was discovered in Great Smoky Mountains National Park. According to Frank Hale at the University of Tennessee, where Johnson did her master's degree in forestry, the hemlocks native to Asia and the western United States seem to be resistant to the adelgid. But the graceful eastern hemlocks, which filter sunlight over rushing streams, are apparently highly susceptible to the adelgid. The nearly microscopic insects—Hale describes them as 1/32 of an inch—attach themselves to the base of the hemlock needles on new twig growth and feed from it. The aphid-like insects are covered with cottony white tufts, giving them the "woolly" appellation. As the adelgids suck the life from the tree, the hemlock's needles turn yellow and drop, its branches dry out and die, and if the infestation is not controlled, in two to six years, depending on its size, the tree will perish.

Already, stands of old-growth hemlock in the Middle Atlantic states have been decimated, and the U.S. Forest Service warns that by 2020 the full range of the eastern hemlock could be infested, from Maine to Georgia and from New Jersey to Michigan. In a report at the end of 2003, Will Blozan of the Eastern Native Tree Society sounded an alarming note. "The great hemlocks of the Southern Appalachians will likely be just a historical anecdote in a few more seasons," he wrote. In her own April 2005 briefing statement on the impacts of forest insects and disease, Johnson put the hemlock woolly adelgid at the top of her hit list. The gift shop at the park's Sugarlands Visitors' Center sells "Save the Hemlocks" T-shirts, and Friends of the Smokies are raising money to fund the fight they hope will prevent Will Blozan's dire prediction from coming true.

There is no question that many of our native trees are already threatened with extinction. "The number of exotic pests is on the increase," Johnson tells me, and they increased "significantly when trade barriers with China and Russia went down in the last decade." Already, the balsam woolly adelgid, an insect from Europe that was the subject of Johnson's master's thesis, has reduced three quarters of the park's once lush Fraser firs to ghostly gray sticks on the higher-elevation slopes of the mountains at Clingman's Dome. Dogwood anthracnose, a fungus introduced to the United States in 1977, is killing the flowering trees that glimmer along streambeds in the park. Johnson's briefing also mentions European mountain ash sawfly, beech scale, the southern pine beetle, and the "infamous" gypsy moth that, in the eastern U.S., feeds primarily on oaks and a few other hardwoods. The Asian long-horned beetle and emerald ash borers pose more potential threats, as does sudden oak death, an Asian fungus that has been killing oak forests on the West Coast and has escaped to the east with nursery shipments from California.

Many if not all of these threats are the result of importing trees and shrubs from overseas, with some of the pests merely hitchhiking on packing material for a host of other products. Johnson feels there is "insufficient emphasis" on the part of border inspectors to prevent

43

infestation of our native forests by the stowaways sneaking into the country. Once a foreign fungus or an exotic insect invades a backyard garden, it can escape to the forest, and as we learned with the chestnut blight of the early twentieth century, it can be devastating. The magnificent American chestnut that once dominated this forest is now only a legend; most people over fifty have never seen one. I have spotted the ragged sproutings of chestnut that grow in forests where old rootstock still exists, but these trees rarely live more than a few years before succumbing to the blight.

The death, regeneration, and succession of trees is a familiar story to foresters, but the eradication of our native trees by an invasion of exotic pests is something else. "If we are going to have native forests in the future," Johnson tells me, "it is imperative to preserve large areas of wilderness. It's in those areas that you're going to find biodiversity." Recognized as one of the most biologically diverse areas in the world, Great Smoky Mountains National Park has been designated as an International Biosphere Reserve by the United Nations. As it was in the ice age, it is home to many different life forms. The park has over four thousand different species of flowering plants, almost a hundred of them considered "endemics," plants that grow only in a specific region. There are 130 different kinds of trees, more than two thousand different fungi, 230 different birds, 67 different mammals, nearly a hundred different reptiles and amphibians, fifty different native fish, and untold numbers of invertebrates. Researchers assisted by a small army of volunteers are working on the All Taxa Biodiversity Inventory, a project designed to survey every species of flora and fauna in the park. So far, ten thousand distinct species have been identified; scientists estimate there may well be as many as a hundred thousand. Over five hundred of those identified so far have never even been heard of before. "Areas like this are increasingly becoming islands surrounded by development," Johnson says, making the management of exotic pests even more important if the Smokies are to remain a refuge for native species like the eastern hemlock.

Hemlocks were once cut for the rich tannic acid content of their bark, which was used in the tanning industry. Today hemlocks are not a particularly valuable tree to the timber industry, so until recently little

44

attention has been focused on protecting them. But hemlocks, which grow up and down the northern slopes of the Appalachians and can live to be over four hundred years old, help to create habitats for brook trout and other fish by cooling the air over streams with their drooping evergreen boughs, and they are the preferred home of warblers, wood thrush, and vireos. So losing the hemlocks could mean another type of silent spring. Johnson is also concerned that if the hemlocks die, the opening of the forest canopy will allow more non-native species of trees to take hold of newly available space open to sunlight. There are no other native evergreens to take the place of hemlocks growing along streambeds. If hemlocks disappear, an entire ecosystem could also cease to exist.

To many people, saving the hemlocks is also simply a matter of aesthetics. With their long, drooping branches and short evergreen needles, hemlocks stitch a delicate tapestry for the eyes. When it rains, their soft, flat needles bead with liquid silver, catching light and holding it in shining droplets. As hemlocks grow tall, their bark takes on a pleasingly rough red patina, and their branches whisper in the wind. Because hemlocks are so important to the beauty of Great Smoky Mountains National Park, workers have been spot-spraying trees in the most widely visited areas of the park's hemlock forests with biodegradable insecticidal soap, and injecting a nicotine-based insecticide called Imidacloprid into the trunks of old-growth trees. For large stands of trees in remote areas, however, these approaches are hardly feasible. Hemlocks cover more than three thousand acres in the park; treating every acre would be an impossibly difficult and expensive task. In the end, the best hope for saving the hemlocks may be another insect, a tiny predator beetle called *Sasajiscymnus tsugae*, known as the "St beetle" for short.

❧

I can't imagine Veronica Gibson wielding a chain saw. She doesn't appear to be more than five feet five inches tall, and with her pretty face framed by smooth, dark hair, she looks as if she would be more at home holding a violin. Yet every weekend at this time of year, she and a team of three other research associates from the University of

Tennessee's Lindsay Young Beneficial Insects Laboratory take chain saws and go out in a pickup truck to scour the countryside looking for hemlock woolly adelgid. They cut down infested trees and bring adelgid-laden hemlock boughs back to the lab for the St beetle to munch. The St beetle will only feed on hemlock woolly adelgid, and scientists hope that breeding the predator beetles here and releasing them into hemlock groves at Great Smoky Mountains National Park will eventually control the adelgid.

Unfortunately, the adelgid isn't too hard to find. Just this morning, Carl Jones, the biologist who administers this lab and others in the university's Department of Entomology and Plant Pathology, says he spotted adelgid on the hemlock trees in his own backyard in nearby Maryville.

Talking with me in his large corner office looking out on the UT campus in Knoxville, Jones, a big, friendly bear of a man, is gloomy about the situation he and his scientists face. "We're losing the hemlocks," he tells me. "If they are untreated we're going to lose ninety-five percent. We're just trying to save as high a percentage as we can." The purpose of the insect-rearing facilities here, he says, is to find safe, biological means of treating infestation problems like these. "This is not the last nasty bug that's coming our way," he says, echoing Kristine Johnson's assessment.

Scientists have been studying the St beetle as a means of biological control for ten years now, and have determined that it is safe to release in the wild—it will not threaten any other native animals or plants. It just goes after the adelgid. The small team here is working feverishly to breed as many as possible. They released twenty thousand beetles in the park last year, and they plan to release a hundred thousand more this summer. Eventually, they hope, the St beetle will take hold in the forest and control the adelgid, creating a natural balance between the hemlocks, the adelgid, and the breeding cycles of predators like itself.

Writing about the dangers of using pesticides in her book *Silent Spring*, Rachel Carson maintained that biological controls were the best way to keep insects in check. Not only would chemicals like DDT decimate the populations of birds and endanger the health of human

46

beings, pesticides would also kill both the pests eating our crops and the predators that feed on the pests, giving the pests the upper hand in the long run. What was needed, she felt, was a more refined awareness of how "nature controls her own." In *Silent Spring*, she wrote:

> *Most of us walk unseeing through the world, unaware alike of its beauties, its wonders, and the strange and sometimes terrible intensity of the lives that are being lived about us. So it is that the activities of the insect predators and parasites are known to few. Perhaps we may have noticed an oddly shaped insect of ferocious mien on a bush in the garden and been dimly aware that the praying mantis lives at the expense of other insects. But we see with understanding eye only if we have walked in the garden at night and here and there with a flashlight have glimpsed the mantis stealthily creeping upon her prey. Then we sense something of the drama of the hunter and the hunted. Then we begin to feel something of that relentlessly pressing force by which nature controls her own.*

Learning to assist nature in controlling her own, rather than destroying pests with dangerous chemicals, Carson believed, was the only long-term solution for human beings to live in harmony with the world and all of its creatures—even the ones that like to eat our crops. She also believed that biological controls were the best way to restore a natural balance to recovering forests, because a forest is more than a collection of trees. Every forest embodies a complex web of interactions between trees and the other creatures that live among them, with them, and on them. When those interactions are disturbed, in even the smallest way, an entire ecosystem can be put at risk.

Down the hall in the UT lab, Ellen Gilch shows me boxes filled with infested hemlock boughs where the St beetles are breeding. She says there "aren't enough hours in the day" for managing the production of the *Sasajiscymnus tsugae* beetles. The St beetles are related to the familiar red and black lady bug beetles we welcome in our gardens, but St is much smaller, and solid black. Holding her finger against one of the clear plexiglass breeding boxes, she points to the tiny beetles flying around inside. They're about the size of an infant's eyelash, and they look eager to get out and start hunting down adelgid in the wild. Along with Nick Reynolds and Margie McKee, Gilch takes care of

47

the beetles, making sure the temperature in their breeding boxes stays between 74 and 76 degrees, the humidity is high, but not too high, and the adelgid is plentiful. As I talk with Gilch, who has a degree in wildlife resource management, I see Reynolds, who has a degree in ecology, going in and out of the lab carrying breeding boxes. McKee, who says she used to be a hairdresser, is smearing honey inside one of the breeding boxes to keep the beetles happy until more adelgid arrive. Down the hall in another lab, Ernie Bernard and Veronica Gibson are preparing "bouquets" of adelgid-infested hemlock boughs to put in the breeding boxes. "This is the most intense lab I've ever worked in," says Bernard, a scientist with a Ph.D. in nematology, when I stop in to take a look. "But it's a good feeling when we release a thousand of these beetles into the park each week." Infestations of adelgid at the park have been mapped, and the beetles are released where they have the best chance of finding their prey and settling in as long-term residents of the forest. The experiment has the potential for stopping the assault on the hemlocks because here, at least, the adelgid has not already destroyed the forest as it has in other places around the country. There is a chance that some of the hemlocks here could still survive.

※

It is mid April in the Smokies, and at Great Smoky Mountains National Park we are having what people in Tennessee call "dogwood weather." Spells of cool, rainy nights and misty mornings alternate with warm, sun-filled days. The dogwood lift up their waxy white flowers like offerings of light, and the redbud trees, more fuschia-colored now than red, make splashes of color along the mountains' lower slopes. The hardwood trees are just beginning to bud; maples blush pink on the hills. The rhododendron are not yet in bloom, but wildflowers blanket the roadsides, taking advantage of the spring sunlight reaching the forest floor through the branches of the hardwood trees. As my husband Bill and I drive through the park, we can see trillium, columbine, and white fringed phacelia. When we stop to explore, we encounter sweet white violets, yellow violets, common blue violets, and dogtooth violets. Bathed continually in mists and rain, the fertile slopes of the Smokies provide a luxurious environment for wild flowers. The valleys here get over fifty inches of rain a year; at the highest elevations, some areas get over eighty-five inches.

The rain comes with a price. Because of their location, wedged between major population areas like Atlanta to the east and the coal-burning power plants to the west, and because of their naturally humid environment, the Smokies attract highly polluted air, especially on the mountaintops. As a result, rainfall here is typically ten times more polluted than, usual, causing stream water to become too acidic for some native fish. Sulfur emissions in the air also cause the blue mists that gave the mountains their name to turn into murky smog. Designated for protection under 1977's Clean Air Act, the park is under constant surveillance, and over the past ten years, the situation has improved. According to air quality specialist Jim Renfro, sulfur dioxide levels at Great Smoky Mountains National Park are down forty percent, nitrogen is not getting worse, and ozone levels are going down. Renfro works hard at long-term monitoring, research, education, and partnerships with industry to try to reduce pollutants that have the potential to damage trees, soil, water, and wildlife. Despite the improvements, Great Smoky Mountains National Park has some of the worst air quality of any of our national parks.

Still, I can't think of anywhere else in the country where I can see so many different native plants and trees. In springtime, this is my favorite place to be. I know I could come back to it year after year for the rest of my life and probably never see it all. I will never know all of the stories these mountains have to tell. I can only imagine how hard it must have been for the Cherokee to leave.

❧

Over the winter, Bill and I have both been ill. Bill suffered a heart attack, and has had three stents implanted in his coronary arteries. I am on medication to control my blood pressure. We've become well acquainted with the emergency room at our hospital back home in Wellsville, and we are on a first-name basis with the staff at the hospital's rehabilitation facilities. So, not for us today the seven-mile hike to the stand of giant virgin hemlock in Albright Grove at the northeastern end of the park. Those trees are infested with adelgid, I'm told, and unfortunately they are already considered a lost cause. Fortunately, there are other places to look at a hemlock forest.

On Wednesday morning, Bill's birthday, we drive up the Roaring Forks Motor Nature Trail to see the forest below Grotto Falls, where Kristine Johnson says we will find plenty of hemlocks. Frothing streams rush down the mountainside through boulder fields along the road—the aptly named "roaring forks." Waterfalls fed by the early morning rain make white veils on the steep, rocky slopes. In the lot at the Grotto Falls trailhead, only a few other cars are parked, along with a red pickup truck attached to a trailer holding a lone llama. The tawny, long-necked creature with its rabbity ears and luminous eyes stands quietly idle in the trailer. Other llamas, I assume, are already on their way up the mountain to the Lodge at Mount LeConte, a hikers' inn accessible only by a steep, five-mile climb. Smaller than horses, sure-footed and calm, a team of llamas carries supplies to the inn on Mondays, Wednesdays, and Fridays, and comes back down again with trash. Why this one has stayed behind I don't know. Perhaps, like us, he's out of shape, or lame, or otherwise not prepared for the four-hour climb up the mountain. Maybe today he's just not in the mood.

The morning began in a soaking rain. Now, the rain has stopped, and the trees are dripping. We walk back down the road from the parking lot and into the hemlock forest, stepping into a wet, green world of filtered light. Hemlock trees' branches are so open and their needles so small that a grove of hemlocks creates a unique kind of shade compared to other evergreens—less shadowy, more airy. Where sunlight reaches the trees, the morning's raindrops glitter like nets of diamonds. "This is definitely old growth," Bill says, pointing to the tall, straight trees towering above us. But there are younger trees here as well, a thriving hemlock community of three or four generations, including grandparents, parents, and children. There is also ghostly evidence of their long-dead ancestors.

As we walk under the trees, we come to a classic pit and mound formation, sign of a large tree that fell a century or more ago, leaving a pit where its roots had been, and a mound where the root ball decayed on the ground. There is no other sign of the tree. There are many old trees still standing, and while they may not be as massive as the four-hundred-year-old giants in Albright Grove, they are nothing to sneer at. I stand beside one of the elders, mesmerized by its mossy bark. The velvety green coating of moss extends up the tree trunk higher than my head, glowing like a living jewel. I wonder how old the moss is, how long it has been growing here. With the patience of a plant that has never counted time, the moss drinks water from the humid air and spreads itself languorously over the bark of the hemlock. In the orient, moss is cultivated as an aesthetic element of a garden. I can understand why. Old woods like this one, with its moss-covered trees and rocks, make an environment suited to contemplation. In the green world of the hemlock woods, the trees are at one with the moss, the moss at one with the rocks, the rocks at one with the mountains, the mountains at one with the rushing streams. And for a few moments, we are at one with the forest.

Fallen trees lie here and there, but nowhere do I see the cottony white tufts of the hemlock woolly adelgid. This grove, for now, at least, is alive and well, young trees taking the place of the ones that have fallen. But the rest of its story is yet to be written. Will *Sasajiscymnus tsugae* become a silent partner here, keeping the adelgid in check and granting a future to hemlock groves like this? Or will woods like this survive only in memory, and legend? I understand now why Veronica Gibson goes out on the weekends armed with a chainsaw. If the effort to save the hemlocks here works, it will be an extraordinary story. It will be one of the rare times when human ingenuity has been employed for the purpose of allowing a forest to remain itself, and permitting nature to control her own.

After meeting our friends Fred and Mary Brenner for a luncheon to celebrate Bill's birthday, Bill, Mary, and I set out to see another type of forest. One reason Great Smoky Mountains National Park is unique is that it is not one forest, but five. In fact, it's often said that by starting at the Sugarlands Visitors' Center, and driving up the Newfound Gap Road to Clingman's Dome, where the Appalachian Trail passes through the park, you can see all five different types of forests that grow from Georgia to Maine. On the dry, lower slopes exposed to sunlight is the pine and oak forest with its thickets of rhododendron, hickory, and dogwood. The hemlock forest grows to elevations of 4000 feet.

Climb to 4,500 feet, and you see the northern hardwood forest, where broad-leaved deciduous trees grow, including beech, birch, and maple. At Clingman's Dome, where the elevation is 6,643 feet above sea level, you can see the spruce-fir forest, an evergreen forest that grows only on mountain peaks.

In between are the cove hardwoods, sheltered valleys with fertile soils where an exceptional variety of both evergreen and deciduous trees congregate, along with a profusion of wildflowers. The "cove" refers to the sheltered basins on hillsides where deep soil has collected to support rich growth. It's Mary's idea that we try the Cove Hardwoods Nature Trail today. My pocket-sized "Day Hikes of the Smokies" guide tells us that the trail will wind through "a magnificent cove hardwood forest" with "one of the best wildflower displays in the mountains each spring." The forests here are large enough to accommodate the browsing deer that destroy wildflowers in other parts of the country. Here in the Smokies, the deer can disperse, and the wildflowers continue to thrive.

To reach the trail, I drive our rental car a few miles up the Newfound Gap Road to the Chimneys Picnic Area across from the bank of the Little Pigeon River. We are still in the Sugarlands, where the pioneer families who lived here tapped the sugar maple trees, giving the place its name. They also farmed the coves, growing corn and potatoes and trading for the rest of what they needed with other mountain families. Now there is a terraced space devoted to picnic tables where modern-day families can bring in packaged lunches. But the rain has begun again, and the picnic tables are empty. I park at the top of the lot, and we pull on rain jackets with hoods. Outside, we find the small sign marking the trailhead and walk up into the woods.

Unlike forests dominated by one or two kinds of trees, the cove hardwoods are a potpourri of different species, including some evergreens. Even the second growth on the lower slope of the cove is quite tall, and as we climb the trail, we pass yellow buckeye, sugar maple, oak, locust, basswood, birch, and tulip trees, a much richer texture of trees than I have ever seen in one place. The soil in these protected coves where the glaciers never came supports such a variety

52

of trees that the forest resembles a kind of horticultural display created by a master gardener.

But there is one thing here you'll never see in a hothouse exhibit— bear claw marks. Like people carving their initials on a tree, bears have left their signatures, scraping long, jagged scars on the bark of some of the yellow buckeyes. The scars look old, but there is no question that bears are about. Five years ago this spring, a fifty year old woman named Glenda Ann Bradley died on the Little River Trail after apparently being attacked by a female black bear, which was found standing over her body. A schoolteacher from Cosby, Tennessee, Bradley was an experienced hiker, but no one was with her when she died, so what caused the bear to attack is unknown. The gift shop at the Sugarlands Visitors' Center still sells cute and cuddly plush bear cub toys, but park newsletters speak of the "unpredictable behavior" of real bears, and warn against disturbing or feeding them. The bear population in the park is growing, and with last year's bumper crop of acorns in the forest for food, a bumper crop of bear cubs is also expected this spring. Some sixteen hundred bears already live in the park, about two per square mile.

A forest is much more than its trees; besides bear, the cove forest is home to woodpeckers, warblers, owls, and wrens. Deer, squirrels, foxes, chipmunks, and mice live here, along with butterflies and snails. Biologists come here to study the park's thirty different types of salamanders—the world's most diverse population. Back home, we find salamanders and newts living in our pond, but here there are also terrestrial salamanders finding shelter in the mossy shadows under the fallen, decaying logs of the forest trees.

As for bear, it is raining too hard now for any self-respecting bear to be prowling about; only Bill and Mary and I are determined to roam the forest in the rain, tilting our heads back to look at the many different trees. We try to identify them by their bark, because most aren't fully leafed out yet. One of the most distinctive trees in the cove forests of the southern Appalachians is the Carolina silverbell, and there are many tall, old specimens here that we can identify by their white-streaked bark and last season's oblong yellow leaves on the ground at our feet. I regret that they are not yet in bloom—we are a few weeks too early to see the pendant white flowers that give the tree its name. Bees love the bell-shaped flowers; squirrels eat the seeds. Crafters use the soft, close-grained wood of the silverbell for carving; furniture makers use its reddish-colored heartwood as a substitute for cherry. The silverbell is a tree I never see up north, but its reputation is spreading among horticulturalists promoting native trees. Hardy and so far free of the pests that plague many ornamental trees, the silverbell is a good candidate for homeowners who want a flowering tree native to our continent. My home in western New York is probably too cold for the silverbell's liking, but a little further south, I think, it would be well worth growing for its show of white blossoms in the spring.

Right now, wildflowers are stealing the spotlight. Like drifts of spring snow, white trillium and white fringed phacelia cover the ground where the hardwood trees have dropped their leaves to make a fertile layer of humus. Sweet white violets grow among the mossy rocks on the ground beneath the tulip trees. Mary finds white foam flower lifting its stalk of tiny flowers from a cluster of low-growing leaves, and I find bellwort, a plant with drooping, bell-shaped yellow flowers like a campanula growing right out of a patch of emerald moss.

And everywhere, there are rocks. The park is strewn with boulder fields, and this forest is no exception. The rocks we see here fell from farther up the mountain during the last ice age, ten thousand years ago. The Appalachians are old and broken mountains, once-jagged peaks worn down to rolling ridges. These rocks are artifacts of the mountain's youth. The people who farmed the coves had to roll many rocks aside before they could plant their corn. Mary spots a farmer's pile of rocks off to the side of a small field where only fern and trillium grow today.

54   At the top of the trail, we can look down the hill and see where the farmers also logged; the forest is coming back, but the trees are smaller, and hemlock grow among the hardwoods. In a steady rain, we walk back down the trail through a grove of young hemlock, and just before we turn toward the parking lot I stop to examine one of the trees. At the base of the twigs on the new green growth is the unmistakable sign of the woolly adelgid, white tufts that look like damp little swabs of cotton in the rain.

CHAPTER FIVE
Giants

The pungent odor of wood smoke permeates the air over the Wawona Road in Yosemite National Park on the day of the summer solstice. The forest floor is black with soot, and scorch marks reach several feet up the trunks of the pines. Among the evergreens, a few hardwood trees here and there are dying, their leaves hanging limp and brown. This is all evidence of a prescribed burn, obviously a very recent one.

When Bill and I stop to inquire at the Visitors' Information Center on the grounds of the old Wawona Hotel, we find a flyer posted telling the whole story. The prescribed burn at Wawona took place exactly a week ago, unbeknownst to us, on the hot, dry day we arrived in San Francisco. A few days later, as we prepared to come to Yosemite, rain falling in the park put the Wawona fire out. Fire managers at the park watch and wait for such conditions, usually in spring and fall, when the tourist season is not in full swing, and they can count on a few dry days followed by a soaking rain. Rain has been frequent here this spring, so heavy several weeks ago that a few of the roads in Yosemite Valley were flooded. The spring rains have fed the foaming waterfalls we've seen the past two days, many of them ephemerals that will disappear once the dry season sets in. Now, the sky over the granite peaks of the Sierras is a bright, clear blue, and along the roadsides purple lupine bloom. But here on the Wawona Road the smell of smoke still lingers.

The Wawona burn covered 367 acres of evergreen forest, mostly ponderosa pine, part of the Park Service plan to restore fire to ponderosa pine ecosystems and to create a fire break for "community protection" around places like the Wawona Hotel. It's a way of fighting fire with fire; allowing brush, fallen branches, and other forest debris to accumulate can make areas of human habitation more susceptible to a dangerous wildfire. The flyer was printed to warn visitors with respiratory problems of the smoky conditions, and to advise everyone traveling through the area to stay away from the fires and use headlights to guide their cars through the smoke. At the Visitors' Center, volunteer Linda Shepler says the air was filled with smoke from the burn all the previous week, and the golfers at the Wawona Hotel weren't happy. Yes, golfers. There is a golf course in Yosemite, and no doubt John Muir would be turning over in his grave to know it.

But besides the golfers there are many people here who love the forest, and after years of fire suppression, they now believe that fire is an important aspect of forest ecology. At the Wawona Visitors' Center, an exhibit lists "The Benefits of Fire." The heat of a fire allows the cones of evergreen trees to open and drop their seeds to the ground. The ground is better prepared to receive the seeds when scrub brush and fallen branches have been cleared away by a fire. Fire releases nutrients in the soil, making it more friable. An inch or two of light, flaky ash is exactly what a tiny sequoia seed needs to germinate. And with competing trees removed, more sun can reach the forest floor to nourish a growing seedling.

Fire can also kill destructive insect populations like carpenter ants, and help to curb the growth of invasive, non-native plants. In the open areas created by fires, wildlife activity increases. Finally, prescribed, controlled burns like this one can reduce the threat of much more devastating wildfires by removing the fuel of dry, fallen branches and leaves that can ignite and burn uncontrollably during periods of drought.

Every year in California, we see wildfires burning out of control, destroying forests, homes, and businesses and threatening both human and animal life. Americans have come to think of fire as a menace, and for well over a hundred years, we avoided it. We *put out* fires with the idea of eliminating them. We *fought* fires as we fight a war, with the idea of achieving victory over an enemy. Now, ecologists say the truth is that fire can actually cleanse and nourish a forest, and might even be a kind of friend. We also know that fire was once much more common and accepted. Some forest fires were started by lightning, just as they are today. But the indigenous people of the North American continent were also fire starters. The Ahwahnechee Indians who lived here in the Yosemite Valley used fire to enlarge meadows and clear areas under oak trees for gathering the acorns the trees produced as a food crop. Galen Clark, who settled here on the south fork of the Merced River in the nineteenth century, reported that the Ahwahnechee used fire to keep the valley "clear of thickets and young trees and brushwood shrubbery so that they could not be waylaid ambushed or surprised by enemies from outside and to not afford biding places for Bears or other predatory animals, and also to have clear ground for gathering acorns which constituted one of their main articles of food." Because of the clearing effect produced by more frequent fires, historians believe that forests all over North America probably looked much more open and park-like at one time than the impenetrable thickets we often find today.

Recognizing its importance, ancient people honored fire and gave it a prominent place in myth and ritual. The burnt offering was a way to communicate with supernatural beings, and sacred fires burned in shrines to the gods. The Celts made bonfires on hillsides and carried flaming torches in procession for their solstice celebrations, honoring the power of the sun. To Native Americans, a fire in the Medicine Lodge represents the dwelling place of the Great Spirit. To Christians, fire symbolizes the presence of the Holy Spirit. We still light candles in our churches, but these tiny flames do little to remind us of a natural force many of us no longer comprehend or appreciate. Fire was once a symbol of the life-giving energy of the sun. Fire purifies and renews, burning away ignorance and delusions to reveal the truth. Yet fire is a maddeningly ambiguous image. Fire can be the warmth and safety of the hearth, or the fearful flames of eternal damnation. Fire is both sexual passion and spiritual fervor. Fire is both death and regeneration.

Fires once raged through the Sierras, but over the last one hundred fifty years, the policy of fire suppression around human settlements created an unprecedented era of fire deprivation for the forest. Nate Stephenson, a forest ecologist with the U.S. Biological Survey, reports that during this time, many sequoia groves in the Sierras failed to reproduce, demonstrating how important fire is to the survival of these unique forests of giant evergreen trees. Stephenson says that

57

the sun-loving sequoias require particularly hot fires to kill other trees competing for water and light, and to open sunny areas in the forest canopy. Yosemite now has a seven-year plan for fire, with 1,817 acres targeted for prescribed burns. Wildfires, if they occur naturally in places where they don't threaten people or park facilities, are allowed to burn in small areas under close supervision.

Fires set by Native Americans in earlier times to clear fields for farming, grazing, hunting, and camping grounds sometimes burned out of control, and the fires set by today's Americans have been known to do the same. At the beginning of May 2000, a prescribed burn at the peak of New Mexico's Cerro Grande Mountain was fanned by unexpectedly high winds and became an inferno. The Cerro Grande fire eventually destroyed over four hundred homes in the Los Alamos area and engulfed some forty-eight thousand acres of forest, giving prescribed burns a very bad reputation. A National Fire Plan now requires tighter controls for prescribed burns. Fire fighters and fire trucks must be on hand to monitor burns like the one at Wawona. And before a prescribed burn can start, the park supervisor must review the condition of fuel on the forest floor, the weather reports, the wind conditions, and the availability of water, fire fighters, and fire equipment. After a prescribed burn is over, a report must be filed to assess the results. Plots at both prescribed burns and wildfires are studied to document the effectiveness of fire in restoring the forest's health.

When Bill and I continue down the Wawona Road, we see evidence of the plan to burn more of the forest. Hundreds of small brush piles have been raked up all over the forest floor, ready to be set ablaze sometime this fall when the tourist season winds down. Such efforts may not exactly replicate the kinds of fires that contributed to forest ecology hundreds of years ago, before the era of hotels, restaurants, and golf courses at Yosemite. But most ecologists think they are better than no fire at all.

58

As we drive along the Wawona Road towards the park's south portal, we are traveling the same route, more or less, taken by Galen Clark when he came here in 1855. Drawn to California, like many before him, by the promise of discovering gold, he was in the gold camps only a short time before he contracted a lung infection so serious that doctors gave him two months to live. He decided to spend his last days in the Sierras. He established a camp near the spot where the Wawona Hotel now stands, on the bank of the south fork of the Merced. Living in the forest he loved restored his health, and two years later, still alive despite the predictions of his doctors, he followed a tip from another prospector and discovered something better than gold—an extraordinary grove of big trees on a hillside seven miles east of his camp. He named the grove Mariposa, for the county of Mariposa to the south.

Many giant sequoia groves were destroyed by logging, despite the fact that the tree's soft, brittle wood shatters when cut and isn't good for much except roof shingles. For some, the challenge of felling such enormous trees was enough incentive to continue logging; others protested the destruction of the giant trees. Thanks to Galen Clark's efforts, the Mariposa Grove was never logged, and along with Yosemite Valley, it was included in the nation's first protected place, set aside by Abraham Lincoln in 1864 for future generations to enjoy. The state of California gave Clark the responsibility of guarding the big trees and paid him a salary of five hundred dollars a year. Clark introduced John Muir and others to the Mariposa Grove of giants, and while he never had Muir's high profile, he wrote three books about Yosemite, and in a quiet, behind-the-scenes way, he promoted both the protection and the popularity of the grove. Muir called Clark "the kindest and most amiable of all my mountain friends" and "one of the most sincere tree-lovers I ever knew." Clark served as "Guardian of Yosemite" for the next twenty years. He encouraged people to visit Yosemite, but I am sure he could never have anticipated how popular a place it would become. Over a million people a year now visit the Mariposa Grove alone.

Millions of years ago, sequoia grew over much of the western half of the continent. Today, there are seventy-five groves left, scattered along a narrow band only fifteen miles wide on the western slopes of the Sierras, between elevations of 5,000 to 7,000 feet, in patches thirty to a hundred miles apart. John Muir tried to find evidence that these sequoia forests were once more continuous in the Sierras, forced to retreat into the isolated groves we see today because of pressure from glaciers, or earthquakes, or drought. But he came to the conclusion, "after long and careful study," meaning weeks of tromping the mountains alone, that these sequoias had never spread out over the slopes of the Sierras as other trees will do. Perhaps that is their secret. They find a spot they like, and they settle in. For a couple of thousand years.

The Mariposa Grove, one of three stands of sequoia in Yosemite, is the largest of the Sierra's sequoia groves, harboring over five hundred of the giant trees. They are rare, they are beautiful, they are extremely tall, and they are extremely old. Sequoias are not the oldest trees on earth—that distinction belongs to the bristlecone pine, some of which are over four thousand years old. Neither are they the tallest trees on earth—that distinction belongs to the coastal redwoods, which grow to be over three hundred feet tall. But the oldest of the giant sequoia are close to three thousand years old, and they are the largest beings on earth by virtue of their volume. The General Sherman tree in Sequoia National Park is 274.9 feet tall, taller than a thirty-story building, and it contains an estimated 52,508 cubic feet of wood. Sequoias grow quickly and reach their mature height after six to eight hundred years. After that, they put on weight, expanding out instead of up, growing bulging layers of cinnamon-colored bark. Their roots spread out around them, as far as a hundred feet or more from the tree, but they are shallow, reaching only a few feet down into the earth, and this can make the trees top heavy, especially after a winter's load of snow. Yet when giant sequoias fall, they do not rot for many centuries. Carbon dating has shown that the enormous tree known as the Fallen Monarch, near the base of the hill at Mariposa Grove, has been lying there intact for well over three hundred years.

When we drive past the park's south portal we are only a few miles from the lower part of the grove. This is not where Galen Clark discovered the giant trees. Probably he hiked along the south fork of the Merced River and up the hill to the vista now called Wawona Point, and there he found the upper grove of the giant sequoia.

We sight our first giant as we round the bend of the road leading into the parking lot at the lower end of the grove. The road curls right past the tree, a titan dwarfing everything in its presence and looking like something from another world, one created by the imagination.

Yet here it is, its soft red bark glowing against the green shadows of much smaller incense cedar and pine behind it. The deeply furrowed cinnamon-colored bark of the sequoia catches light as it rises from a gently bulging base through the understory of trees around it, and the effect is nothing short of magical.

In the lower grove, a number of these giants share space with more incense cedar and ponderosa pine. At an elevation of 5,600 feet, the air is cool and scented with the resinous perfume of the pine. During the tourist season, a tram runs from the base of the hill to the upper grove, where a replica of Galen Clark's cabin serves as a museum. Many of the people who come to see the big trees park their cars in the lot at the base of the hill and explore some of the trees in the lower grove. A few people make the six-hour trek up to the top of the hill and back down again. We opt for the middle way of taking the tram to the upper grove and then walking down through the forest to the bottom of the hill.

The tram climbs the hill past the Fallen Monarch and the four beautiful sequoias known as the Bachelor and the Three Graces. The huge tree called the Bachelor stands apart from three more slender, graceful trees standing close together nearby. The Bachelor bears a number of black scorch marks, evidence of ancient fires. Fire rarely kills a sequoia once the tree reaches this size, both because the bark may be several feet thick, and because it is rich in tannin and low in resin, retarding burning. A particularly intense fire can burn up from the ground into the base of a giant sequoia, even so far as to hollow it out all the way to the crown, but the tree can go on living for hundreds of years. Analysis of fallen, fire-scarred trees in the Mariposa Grove shows that before the arrival of European settlers, fires burned here as frequently as once a year, with a few fire-free periods lasting as long as fifteen years. Many of the trees in the grove have triangular black scars from past fires, some deep enough to open gaps in the base of the tree.

The famous Wawona Tunnel tree in the upper grove was hollowed out further from one of these gaps to make a tunnel for wagons and later cars to drive through, and became a popular tourist attraction. The tree already had a lean; cutting into it to make a tunnel probably

61

weakened it more than the fire had, and over the winter of 1969, a heavy snowfall finished the job. The huge tunnel tree fell, fortunately when no cars full of tourists were lined up to make their way through. Now, the tram we are riding on and a few official Park Service trucks are the only vehicles permitted on the road.

Giant trees do fall here; in the lower grove, in fact, two sequoias that were each nearly three hundred feet tall came down at the end of February in 2003. They have been left on the trail, cross-sectioned so that visitors can walk right through them. Park officials think a stream passing under one of the sequoias might have caused damage to the tree's shallow root system. The ground let go, and the top-heavy tree fell, taking another nearby tree down with it. The thousand-year-old giants came crashing down in the night, when no humans were there to witness the event or to be in the path of the falling trees. How this continues to happen without people being hurt is a mystery. Maybe the trees wait for a time when people aren't around. I wouldn't be surprised. A tree that has lived for a thousand years must know a thing or two about timing.

Further up the hill is evidence of another prescribed burn where foresters are restoring conditions for the sequoia to regenerate. This looks less recent than the one at Wawona, probably one of last year's burns. There is no smoke in the air, but charred, blackened branches lie on the ground, and the trunks of young trees stand bare of their needles and gray with ash. A sooty, jagged stick of a tree that lost its top in the fire stands out among the others, many of them white firs. Once, I might have looked on this scene as one of devastation and loss. Now I know that the number of shade-tolerant white fir growing up under the sequoia must be reduced if the giant sequoia is to continue growing here as it has in the past. And the tiny sequoia seeds will only sprout when they fall on bare, sunny, friable soil, the kind created by fire. In the Mariposa Grove, fire is used on a regular basis to give sequoia seeds optimum conditions for germination.

A giant sequoia produces abundant seed cones on branches high in the crown of the tree. A mature tree makes two thousand cones a year, and each cone holds an average of two hundred seeds. So potentially, each tree could release four hundred thousand seeds a year. With

62

hundreds of giant sequoia here producing millions of seeds, making new trees should not be difficult. But the sequoia holds onto its cones; the green, egg-shaped cones are tightly scaled and full of sap, so they do not turn brown and dry out on the tree as they would on other evergreens, and they do not release those millions of seeds easily. Some seed cones are torn from the trees by wind and snow. But there are other natural processes at work to assist the giant trees. As in any forest, a relationship of cooperation exists between the trees and the creatures that live among them.

Coexisting with the giant trees are two comparatively miniscule creatures that help to open the sequoia's cones and distribute its seeds. The chickaree, a small tree squirrel common to the Sierra forests, climbs the giant sequoia, cuts the tight green cones from the tree's branches, and feeds on the cone scales, letting the seeds drop to the ground. The chickaree doesn't hibernate, so to get through winter it also caches sequoia cones, sometimes hundreds of them. Inevitably, the chickaree doesn't need every cone it caches, and probably forgets where some of them are. Cones left behind by the chickaree dry out, eventually, and spill their seeds.

The long-horned wood-boring beetle is another creature that helps to disperse the giant sequoia's seeds in a unique way. The female lays her eggs in the cones, and when the beetle larvae hatch, they chew their way out, opening the cones and allowing the seeds to release. In this way, one of the tiniest of nature's creatures works together with a giant. Fire speeds up the process, providing the heat necessary to dry and open the green, sap-laden sequoia cones, and paradoxically, fire renews the soil's thirst to retain the moisture a growing seedling requires. During the years of fire suppression, new sequoia seedlings were rare in the grove, but now that the role of fire has been restored, they are beginning to reappear, insuring that in the new millennium, the Mariposa Grove will continue to be a living forest, and not just a tree museum visited by busloads of tourists.

The fate of the Giant Sequoia National Monument south of here, however, has been challenged. Giant sequoia groves in national parks are off limits to logging, but the Bush administration has tried to authorize logging at the Giant Sequoia National Monument, claiming

63

that cutting trees would protect nearby communities from catastrophic fires. The plan would have allowed 7.5 million board feet of timber to be cut from the forest every year. Any healthy tree up to thirty inches in diameter, including sequoia and redwood, could have been cut in order to thin the forest. Even if the larger trees were not cut, logging trucks and the bulldozers used to make roads for them would endanger the fragile ecosystems of these forests of giants.

And without fire, the specific conditions necessary for giant sequoias to reproduce wouldn't exist.

The 327,800 acres of the Giant Sequoia National Monument were not originally included under the protection of the National Park Service, but in 2000, President Clinton proclaimed these acres off limits to logging, a protection the second President Bush's plan eliminated. The Bush plan also eliminated the requirement for logging companies to file environmental impact statements or allow sufficient time for public comment on them before cutting trees. There are thirty-four groves of giant sequoia here, harboring half of the giants in existence, and environmentalists—horrified that the trees were in danger—filed suit against the federal government to stop the logging. The Sierra Club joined with other environmental groups to fight the Bush plan, insisting that the forests in the Giant Sequoia National Monument come under the protection of the Park Service and be managed with carefully monitored prescribed fires and hand removal of brush as they are at Yosemite and at Sequoia and Kings Canyon National Parks. In September 2005, Judge Charles Breyer issued an injunction stopping the logging, which had already begun. Appeals by the timber industry went on for three years.

John Muir believed the only way to protect places like Yosemite and the Mariposa Grove was by granting them the status of national parks. Since his time, some think our national parks are being loved to death, with millions of tourists and their automobiles creating traffic jams. But without the same protection afforded to Yosemite, the fate of the Giant Sequoia National Monument had to be decided in the courts when the timber industrysuspended their appeals—for the time being, at least—-in June 2008. It's possible John Muir had the right idea after all.

Mariposa means butterfly in Spanish, and I am hoping to see some here in the Mariposa Grove of giant sequoia at Yosemite National Park. I am not disappointed. When we get off the tram at the top of the hill and I wander out under the trees, I am greeted by a fluttering Painted Lady, a butterfly with wings that look as if they are splattered with droplets of orange and black paint.

A replica of Galen Clark's cabin stands in the same clearing where he built the original in 1864, surrounded by sun-splashed sequoias. To live among these giants, I think, would be a blessing. Defying the odds given him by the medical profession, Clark lived to a great old age, dying peacefully in his sleep a few days short of his ninety-sixth birthday. During his years in Yosemite, he must have been lonely at times, and probably craved the company of the people he encouraged to visit the Mariposa Grove. Yet I am sure that he must have also been very happy here, and if it is possible for the essence of a human being to remain in a place, then Galen Clark is here, in the trees, in the breeze, in the butterflies' wings. He never struck gold, never became wealthy, never wielded power over the affairs of men, but he found his El Dorado here, in the presence of giants, and like the trees, he lived longer than most men. His days were rich: he saw the peaks of the Sierras glow with the gold of the setting sun, and watched the stars shine silver in the evening sky. The millions of people who come here leave Yosemite knowing his story. How many men of his generation can say the same?

The giant sequoia count time not in days, nor in seasons, nor in years, but in centuries. A young tree, in its infancy, a few hundred years old, has a tall, narrow trunk, and its branches tip up to make a tapered outline, a spear reaching straight for the sky. As it reaches its full height of two hundred feet or more, the tree loses its lower branches, and those above droop down with their flat fronds of evergreen foliage against the cinnamon-colored bark of the trunk. Lightning may strike down a sequoia's branches, but once the tree reaches its mature height and develops layers of bark several feet thick, if it has a reliable supply of water it can easily live another thousand years.

65

The tree called the Grizzly Giant in the lower grove is one of these long-lived titans. It stands 209 feet tall, and since its top branches have likely been struck by lightning and broken off, it was probably once even taller. Its trunk is 90 feet around, 34.7 feet in diameter at its base. Like so many of the sequoia here, it bears several charred, triangle-shaped scars, evidence of fires that might have burned a thousand years ago. Its bark looks gnarled, bumpy, ragged, and rough, the outer layer worn away at the base to a smooth gray, resembling stone. John Muir was hard-pressed to estimate the age of such a tree. He thought some of the giant sequoia might be five thousand years old, or more. Until recently, the best guess of modern scientists was that the Grizzly Giant was twenty-seven hundred years old. Based on his analysis of fallen trees in the grove, Nate Stephenson thinks it might be more like eighteen hundred years. A number of the Grizzly Giant's thick lower branches are broken off. The first one still bearing foliage is eighty-four feet from the ground, and by itself it is six feet in diameter, bigger than the entire trunk of any mature tree I've seen east of the Mississippi. There is no doubt that conditions in the west favor bigger and longer-lived trees than any species we see in the east. An absence of hurricanes and tornadoes here gives trees a chance to survive far past the four or five hundred year limit for most eastern trees; so does the longer growing season. Still, a tree that has lived for eighteen hundred years or more is hard to fathom.

"It doesn't seem real," Bill says, circling the tree with his camera, trying to find an angle where his lens can take it in. "You can never photograph the whole tree." Many people have tried. Galen Clark was photographed standing in front of the Grizzly Giant in 1858; the base of the tree alone takes up the entire background in the shot. It's possible to find a spot downhill from the tree where you can look up and see the whole tree in your lens, but then you lose all the detail. Some photographers use a telephoto lens and just picture the tree's crown filling the frame. Yosemite's many wonders are tantalizingly difficult to capture on film, and the big trees are no exception. Their enormity can be experienced, but reducing that experience to a mere two-dimensional image is impossible. You just have to be there.

It might be easier, Bill says, to set up an easel and spend time transferring images of these trees from eye to canvas with the artist's alchemy. In 1932, Mary Curry Tresidder, who grew up in Yosemite and died in her suite at the Ahwahnee Hotel in 1970, did her best to describe the sequoia with words, in her book *The Trees of Yosemite*. "Aside from the mantle of the centuries," she wrote, "the Giant Sequoia has a claim to reverence by virtue of its beauty, its dignity, its majesty. The pines and firs about it represent an even older family of trees, but the Giant Sequoia dominates and subdues them into a background for itself, a scale from which its greatness may be appreciated. It is not merely an ordinary tree raised to the nth power, but it is the apotheosis of a tree." In other words, the sequoia comes close to being divine. Philosopher Belden Lane says trees like the sequoia have Buddha nature, the capacity to become enlightened beings, undisturbed by desires, distractions, or delusions. They have already acquired the wisdom to live in harmony with their surroundings for thousands of years, making them nearly immortal.

Wandering along the trail that winds down into the lower grove, I decide to try to know the sequoias another way, by using my sense of touch. Water trickles along in small streams throughout the grove, providing the giant sequoias with the surface moisture they need for their shallow roots. I cross a bridge over one of these streams, find a big tree growing near a well-watered spot, and approach it. Placing my hands lightly on the sequoia's trunk, I touch the surprisingly soft, dry bark, which feels more fragile than I expected. With my fingertips, I listen for a moment, waiting. What I sense must be translated into a word I understand—one word: *health*. The tree pulses with health. Health is something I have been praying for, for Bill and I both. Today, on the summer solstice, the longest day of the year, the sequoia pulses with the sacred fire of sunlight, the gift of life, of *health*.

I turn from the tree to find two women in sun visors, tank tops, shorts, and fanny packs huddled together, staring at me and whispering. Maybe they think I shouldn't be touching the tree. They're probably right. Or maybe they think I've lost my senses. If that's what they think, I can't say I blame them. But I think I've actually found my senses. I think I know how Galen Clark was healed, living with giants, keeping their secret ceremonies intact.

CHAPTER SIX
Going Wild

The sky over Warren, Pennsylvania, is bright blue on Sunday, August 7, and church bells ring across town as I stand outside on West Third Avenue. The bells ring today for the Christian Sabbath, but I know that for the ancient Celts the beginning of August was the time of Lughnassadh, a festival honoring the sun god. Most of us recognize the dates of the summer solstice, now six weeks past, and the autumn equinox, six weeks away. But the "cross quarter" times like this one on the ancient Celtic calendar were of even greater importance because they marked the times "in between" the four seasonal markers of the summer and winter solstices and the spring and autumn equinoxes. "In-between" times, whether they fell in between seasons, days, or hours, and including in-between places—like dusk at the seashore, for instance—were times of mystery, as the power of one thing gave way to the other. At the in-between times, energies are being transferred, light is changing, the earth is moving, and now, at the time of Lughnassadh, emphasis is shifting from a time of growth to a time of harvest. The first fruits of the field are coming in, and yesterday the booths at the farmers' market were full of the tempting delights that could be the gifts of the sun god—corn, tomatoes, zucchini, and blueberries, all freshly picked, full of color, plump and shiny with life.

A dark red hatchback pulls up to the curb where I am waiting, and Kirk Johnson gets out to greet me. Johnson has agreed to be my guide today on one of the many trails through the Allegheny National Forest. Executive Director of an organization of citizens calling themselves Friends of Allegheny Wilderness, Johnson is working with the national Forest Service, elected representatives, and the people of the local communities to reach a consensus on designating wilderness areas in the Allegheny National Forest, Pennsylvania's only national forest. The Forest Service is reviewing its fifteen-year management plan, and the Friends would like to see more of the Allegheny National Forest designated as "untrammeled" wilderness, places where hunting, fishing, hiking, and camping could still go on as always, but roads would be banned, along with timber cutting or drilling for oil and gas. Kirk Johnson and the Friends are also frequently finding themselves in between—caught between the interests of groups like the Allegheny Defense Project, who advocate banning all timber cutting or oil exploration in the forest, and those like the Allegheny Forest Alliance, who want to keep all of the forest's riches available for use and preserve as many jobs as they can for the timber industry. The Friends of Allegany Wilderness, says environmental historian Jay Turner, are treading "a middle way," avoiding the extremes of either approach. Writing in the *Erie Time-News* earlier this year, Turner praised this moderate approach and its promise of providing "a compromise that protects our region's natural heritage and its economy."

The importance of this forest to the local economy is exactly what has made managing its resources a complicated task in modern times. The resource-rich Allegheny National Forest comprises 513,000 acres in northwestern Pennsylvania, and so far only nine thousand acres have been designated wilderness, less than two percent of the total. Nationally, about eighteen percent of national forest gets wilderness protection, much of it in the west. But even in the densely populated Northeast, most national forests protect around ten percent. In a meticulously researched proposal, Johnson and the Friends have identified 54,460 acres out of the Allegheny National Forest's 513,000 that they think should receive wilderness status. Their proposal accounts for a little over ten percent of the total acreage, which would bring this area in line with other national forests in the northeast region. They have produced an impressive document illustrated with Kirk Johnson's beautiful photographs of the forest with the intention of convincing the public, the timber industry, the Forest Service, and ultimately the U.S. Congress that these areas should be protected under the 1964 Wilderness Act, while still allowing logging and drilling on ninety percent of the forest.

70

Johnson thinks there is room for both timber cutting and wilderness, and he is careful to say so. "It's not a black and white issue," he tells me. "There are ways for everyone to have their interests represented." Still, he is determined to keep the idea of wilderness areas in the Allegheny National Forest alive. He has gathered support from organizations like the Wilderness Society, the Sierra Club, Trout Unlimited, the Pennsylvania Native Plant Society, the Keystone Trails Association, and many others to endorse the idea of creating more wilderness here. Editorials in newspapers across western Pennsylvania and even in western New York have supported the proposal.

So far, however, the Forest Service is considering only two of the proposed wilderness areas and one recreation area, making up less than half of the acreage the Friends have recommended for wilderness. In its initial survey, the Forest Service rejected wilderness protection for the Tionesta Research and Scenic Area, site of an important old-growth forest awarded a place on the Natural Registry of the National Landmarks program in 1973. The Tionesta area was named one of the nation's "Twelve Treasures in Trouble" in last year's report by the Campaign for America's Wilderness. Ultimately, the decision will be made by Congress. Only an act of Congress can create a wilderness area. But the Forest Service recommendations will carry weight with elected officials.

I find it ironic that the one state with *sylva*, the Latin word for "woods," in its name has done so little to protect its native forests. "Penn's woods," after all, was once home to a great forest, rich in plentiful trees, abundant wildlife, and pristine waterways. Historically, however, these riches have proved irresistible, and as a result few forests on earth have been so thoroughly exploited. Valuable white pine lured the timber industry to western Pennsylvania and generated a frenzy of clear cutting in the late nineteenth and early twentieth centuries, when railroads made transporting the logs of the great trees to market easy and fast. Clear cutting was followed by catastrophic wildfires, and then the chestnut blight, leaving the hillsides bare. But there were still fortunes to be made. The lumber boom gave way to an oil boom after the nation's first oil well was drilled at Titusville in 1859, and since then hundreds of millions of barrels of oil have been

71

removed from the region. Deposits of oil and gas created by pockets of decaying organic material in the sandstone and shale at the bottom of an ancient sea continue to yield riches for today's economy, especially when the price of petroleum exceeds a hundred dollars a barrel. A large refinery operates by the river on the outskirts of Warren, and another north of here in Bradford. Years ago, when I lived in Bradford, I often saw pumpjacks operating in a next-door neighbor's yard, or behind the local McDonald's. Independent oil producers in the region continue to drill wherever they can, and the forest is no exception. There are eight thousand wells in the Allegheny National Forest, two thousand of them drilled in the past few years—more oil wells than exist in all the other national forests in the country combined.

As a result of all this activity, the green hills we see today in western Pennsylvania are nearly all second growth, mainly hardwood forests that grew up after the evergreens had been logged. In addition, the forest has been managed in recent years to favor the black cherry, a valuable tree for making furniture and wood veneer. So what the timber industry likes to call "healthy forest management" is mainly about the market value of trees, not the intricate interrelationships between trees, air, water, and the wild flora and fauna of a region. Dr. Marc Abrams, a forest ecologist at Penn State University, says that an ecological cycle here has been broken; the landscape of Pennsylvania has been completely transformed, and may never fully recover its original character, despite the many trees we see around us now. There is no doubt that this is a very different forest than the one named after William Penn. But it is still a great and beautiful forest, and there are many who think it is worthy of protection. The question is how much, and where.

"It's nice to finally have this bridge open," Kirk Johnson says, sipping coffee from a paper cup as we leave downtown Warren and cross the Allegheny River on the bridge that has just opened for traffic after a two-year renovation project. The river lies gleaming in the sun, a broad ribbon of water edged by green hills. All of the streams in the Allegheny National Forest feed into this river, and one of the reasons the forest here is so important is that it protects the entire Allegheny River watershed. Technology has proven no match for forests in providing clean drinking water to human populations. As enlightened communities all over the world now realize, preserving forests is much more efficient and cost effective than building billion-dollar water-treatment plants. A forest is like a gigantic sponge; trees collect rainwater in their leaves and release it slowly to the ground, keeping water available and flowing at a steady pace. In a wild forest, where pesticides, herbicides, and fertilizers aren't in use and there is no industrial waste, the water is clean and free of pollutants. Tree roots and leaf litter in a forest hold the ground and reduce erosion, preventing floods. Trees also provide shade over streams, keeping water cool. Cutting down trees to build roads for logging and mineral extraction cuts down on the forest's ability to provide clean water. The increasing fragmentation of forests, especially in the densely populated Northeast, makes sources of clean drinking water more and more difficult to find.

The Allegheny is also the river of my dreams. I was born within sight of it, in the city of Pittsburgh, where the Allegheny and Monongahela meet to form the Ohio. For over fifty years now, I have followed this river, drawn to its curving course just as the Seneca Indians, the French trappers, and the British colonists were. As much as any road map, the Allegheny gives me direction and a way to orient myself in the landscape. In many ways, I wouldn't know where I am in either place or time without it. Its source is up near the New York State border, not far from where I live now, and it crosses the border just as I have and meanders for a while through New York before turning back down into Pennsylvania, traversing nearly the entire western frontier of the state before ending its course in Pittsburgh. The Seneca used a secret "Forbidden Trail" a few miles from my home in Wellsville to reach the Allegheny for making expeditions west. After the American Revolution the river became an important trading route, carrying first timber, then coal barges, until railroads took over the job of carrying off the forest's riches. Now we are seeing one of the older forms of

73

transportation again on the Allegheny. In a few days, a national canoe competition will come to Warren for the second time. I'm sure that the forest surrounding the town and its river are part of the allure.

Leaving the river behind, we turn right on Pleasant Road, where the housing lots gradually get bigger, then give way to fields, and finally to forest. Four miles outside Warren is a sign reading "Entering Allegheny National Forest, U.S. Department of Agriculture, Forest Service." We're on Route 337 now, climbing the ridge top over the river. One of the areas that the Friends of Allegheny Wilderness have proposed for protection under the 1964 Wilderness Act is an extension of the Hickory Creek wilderness area where we are headed today. Kirk Johnson says it has some interesting features that I might enjoy seeing. The three areas that the Forest Service is considering recommending for wilderness designation are: Chestnut Ridge, where American Chestnut trees not yet affected by the blight have been growing for as long as twenty years; Tracy Ridge, a largely undisturbed area along the Allegheny Reservoir behind Kinzua Dam, where bald eagles have established nests; and the Minister Valley recreation area south of the old-growth forest at Heart's Content. The Forest Service has declared some of the other areas proposed for wilderness protection unacceptable because of a tangle of bureaucratic rulings, including a controversial "buffer zone" directive issued by the regional forester in Milwaukee back in 1997. The directive states that in order to be considered wilderness, an area must total at least twenty-five hundred acres exclusive of a half-mile buffer zone from any roads. The proposed addition to the Hickory Creek Wilderness where we are going today, at 1,780 acres, doesn't qualify, although it would enlarge the original Hickory Creek Wilderness area approved in 1984 and protect the creek's headwaters. Hickory Creek, a state-designated "Exceptional Value" stream, has a high biodiversity rating in part because it is home to the native brook trout that are increasingly rare in the wild. There is nothing in the original Wilderness Act about the need for buffer zones, and many people contest the 1997 ruling, but Forest Service planners in Warren say they are stuck with it.

We pass the Rocky Gap ATV trail, and a little over ten miles out of town we reach a fork in the road and leave Route 337, bearing left on the road towards Heart's Content. A half mile or so before the Heart's Content Scenic Area, Johnson locates the sign marking the Tanbark Trail, and finds a place to pull off the road and park. The trail crosses the road here; Johnson leads me to the trailhead on the northwestern side of the road—a spot half-hidden by trees and not easy to see—and we walk into the forest, following the off-white, diamond-shaped plaques on the trees that mark the trail.

What we find is a secondary-succession forest of hardwoods and hemlock, trees that grew up after the great clear-cut logging era, the forty years between 1890 and 1930 when railroads made possible fast, large-scale, unsustainable harvesting of timber all over western Pennsylvania. Most of the region's white pine was cut down then. Today we see hundred-year-old red oak, white oak, black cherry, beech, and maple that have succeeded the pine, along with some hemlock, the shade-tolerant trees that must have given this trail its name—their bark was used in the tanning industry. On either side of the trail is glossy mountain laurel, which I imagine will be gorgeous in springtime bloom. On the forest floor is a lush green sea of hay-scented ferns. The ferns are beautiful, filling the air with their characteristic perfume of newly mown hay, but Johnson says their "omnipresence" is not a good sign for the forest. Ferns are the one thing deer won't eat, and their abundance indicates that browsing deer have eliminated other types of plants and trees. Foresters are so concerned about the problem of deer browsing that many have been lobbying the Pennsylvania Game Commission to provide for more thinning of the deer herd, something that hunters don't favor, because having fewer deer makes hunting them more difficult. Unrestricted hunting nearly extirpated deer by the beginning of the twentieth century, and the elimination of browsing deer allowed some of the older trees we are seeing around us to thrive. But once predators like cougar and wolves were also eliminated, and the deer came back with no natural enemies to keep them in check, they have proliferated to the extent that they are preventing the forest from regenerating, a problem I have been hearing about over and over everywhere I go in the Northeast. The problem is particularly acute in Pennsylvania, where the Game Commission, funded by income from hunting licenses, has come under attack for catering to hunters.

75

"This trail is very rocky," I say as I negotiate the stones at my feet. Speaking to me over his shoulder as he goes ahead of me on the trail, Johnson explains that we're walking on the ridge top's sedimentary rock. It's not long before the rocks get bigger and we start to see the monolithic, moss-covered boulders that are one of the promised interesting features on this trail. The enormous boulders are four, six, and sometimes as much as ten feet tall, scattered on either side of the trail like the broken teeth of giants. These sandstone rocks were not thrown down from peaks like the boulders at the Great Smoky Mountains National Park. Johnson says they are the worn-down, exposed remnants of the ridge top itself. Millions of years ago they were at the bottom of an ancient sea, formed by millennia of sediment.

About a half mile from the road, we "thread the needle" by picking our way down a narrow path on a steep slope between two huge slabs of sandstone that tower above us on either side. The loggers may have taken most of the virgin timber from this forest, but they could not move these rocks. To keep from falling, I steady myself with my hands on the mossy, lichen-encrusted boulders of sedimentary rock, touching the stones born of that ancient sea. As we make this passage we are walking through layers of history, going back in time to an experience of the natural world far removed from the life of the town just a few miles away. When we come out on the other side of this rocky passageway I wonder how many people in Warren realize that they live and work so close to so wild a place. We think of wilderness as something remote and inaccessible and far from the civilized world, yet the truth is that this place is only a short distance from a bustling town of banks, bridges, churches, grocery stores, hospitals, hotels, and restaurants, not to mention an oil refinery.

At the bottom of the slope beneath the passageway between the boulders, we come to a small footbridge over Hickory Creek. "We're not far from the source of the creek," Johnson says as we stand on the bridge. "I've followed it upstream to where it rises from a spring." In the water below, he points to the stream bed's gravel, made of the same sedimentary rocks we have just passed through, worn down to the size of pebbles. This is the million-year life cycle of sedimentary stone, born of water, and returned to water. Forest streams like this with graveled bottoms are the preferred habitat of the beautiful and elusive brook trout. With its incandescent orange belly, the yellow and red spots on its dark green back, and the blue halos on its midsection, the brook trout flashes through cool, shallow streams, dazzling the eyes of any beholder. If you've seen one, you are very lucky. Wild brook trout can thrive only in the clean, cool water of a stream shaded by forest trees, and they die out quickly if faced with competition from larger brown trout or rainbow trout stocked in streams by game commissions. It's no wonder that Trout Unlimited has joined the Friends of Allegheny Wilderness in endorsing this part of the forest for wilderness protection. Anglers prize such places for the rare experience of finding fish like the "brookies" alive in their native habitat.

This place was also once a Seneca hunting ground. I know that from reading about it, but I also feel it, as I always feel the silent presence of the Seneca people in the woodlands of western Pennsylvania. I follow in their footsteps on this trail, as I do on any trail I take through this forest. They are like a pentimento, an original image, that has been painted over. Later, much later, when the top layer of paint on a canvas fades and becomes transparent, the original image can be seen again. It is like that with the Seneca. Their land was taken from them, their image on it nearly obliterated; even the sacred ground of their graveyard was desecrated when Kinzua Dam was built to create the Allegheny Reservoir between here and Bradford. Today, up on the Seneca reservation in New York's southern tier, the keepers of the western door announce their presence with a sprawling casino, neon signs glowing by the freeway at all hours of the day and night. But here, in the forest, the stones remember the people who honored creation with ceremonies marking the seasons and cultivated a much closer relationship with the natural world than we enjoy today. I walk with the original Seneca now.

77

Kirk Johnson tells me the stone outcroppings provided overhangs in places that made natural shelters for Seneca hunting parties roaming these woods. As we climb up from the creek I smell wood smoke, and we come in sight of one of these outcroppings being used in almost the same way as it was five thousand years ago. Today, three small tents are pitched in front of a twenty-foot-high wall of rock. One of the young hikers who has pitched his tent here is sitting silently with his eyes closed in front of a small fire. I hope he's meditating, and not just stoned out of his mind. On the wall of rock over his head, modern-day men have not been able to resist the urge to carve their names. "Mike" has been here; so has "Brad." Someone else has carved the words "make love not war."

Skirting the campers and their tents, we climb up into a clearing under the rocks where some smaller boulders provide a sort of natural seating area. Johnson changes the battery in his digital camera and takes a few photographs of the rocks before we both find perches on moss-covered boulders. I pull out my notebook and Johnson pulls out his water bottle and takes a drink. With his dark hair, his bluish gray eyes, and his quiet manner, he has the air of someone who has long lived in tune with the wild. I ask him to tell me why places like this should be protected as wilderness. "I think you can break it down into three main categories," he responds. First, he explains, areas like this one provide permanent refuges for natural flora and fauna, areas that will always be available in their natural condition. "The second reason is for people," he says. "Because the landscape is so heavily developed, and there is so much urban sprawl, we need to preserve the last vestiges of wilderness as an essential part of the human experience."

Behind us, the campers are stirring, and we hear a chorus of howls, followed by laughter. As if on cue, the campers are getting wild. "Wilderness is intended for those seeking a truly primitive outdoor experience," say the Forest Service trail guides. I suppose everyone has their own way of defining "primitive."

The third reason, Johnson continues, is for scientific study. "In forest land where there isn't development, most of the forest is managed for timber production. We need scientific reference areas where natural processes can move forward unaltered." Over a hundred scientific research studies have been written about the Tionesta old-growth area alone. Johnson wrote his master's thesis on the recreational and ecological potential of the Allegheny National Forest. He tells me that archaeologists are studying this area and others in the forest for evidence of the first human settlements here. A botanist named Thomas Rooney from the University of Wisconsin is studying the

78

sensitive native plants growing on the tops of the rocks, which provide a refuge from browsing deer. Presumably, the campers behind us are not doing any research, except perhaps on hallucinogenic substances, but if that's the case I guess it's their business. After a few more gleeful howls, they quiet down.

Johnson smiles at the campers' antics and resumes his answer to my question. Wilderness areas also increase property values, he explains. "Proximity to wilderness is a significant reason people remain in an area," he says. Quality of life is obviously much higher where the scenic value of the landscape is preserved. Given the choice, in other words, no one wants to live surrounded by the devastation of strip mines or hills cut bare of their trees and strewn with ragged stumps.

A less tangible relationship exists between the people of the earth and the wilderness, say some scholars. Ecopsychologists believe that as creatures of the earth we inherently crave a relationship with natural places, and we are healthier and happier when we live within reach of wild forests, rivers, and mountain peaks, even if we only see them outside our windows. Denying our connection with the landscape leaves us feeling isolated and helpless, says Harvard psychologist Sarah Conn. "Most of us in this culture are taught to experience ourselves as bounded, masterful, self-contained individuals who are separate from a dead, inert world which we are supposed to control," says Conn, writing for *Ecopsychology On-line*. "This restricted identity can manifest itself as a lack of community, a lack of meaning, purpose and sense of belonging, as well as ignorance and apathy about environmental degradation." Theodore Roszak, author of *The Voice of the Earth: An Exploration of Ecopsychology*, has advanced the theory that at the very core of our consciousness is an ecological awareness, a psychological heritage passed down from our primitive ancestors, which, if denied or repressed, results in neurosis. Studying the natural processes of the earth, like those that go on in a forest, says Roszak, has also replaced theology for some people. This, in other words, he says, is "where god used to be."

I ask Johnson about the value of protecting forests like this one that are becoming old growth. "In the eastern United States," he says, "one aspect of wilderness preservation is the re-emergence of old-growth forest. If we protect large tracts of land, in time, through natural succession processes, old-growth forests will re-emerge." Old-growth forests are the most biologically diverse forests, he says, despite what those who advocate forest management sometimes claim. Managing a forest by clearing away older trees or favoring some species of trees over others can increase the timber harvest or provide more game like deer and grouse, making the forest look as if it's more productive, but true biodiversity means having as many different species native to a region as possible, including mosses, lichens, and invertebrates a hunter wouldn't necessarily notice. Mosses, lichens, and invertebrates thrive as much on the large woody debris of fallen and older trees as they do on younger trees or the kind of trees valued by the timber industry. And even mosses, lichens, and invertebrates could prove to be of value to someone. "You never know what benefit some unknown species will bring to humans," Johnson says. The cancer-fighting drug taxol, quinine to combat malaria, and common aspirin to ease pain and thin the blood of deadly clots are just a few of the better-known drugs derived originally from forests around the world. Recently, pharmaceutical companies have gone to the forests of Madagascar to study the rosy periwinkle, a tropical shrub that produces two substances found to be effective in treating Hodgkin's disease and childhood leukemia. Plants like these have evolved over thousands of years, developing survival strategies in the wild that can sometimes aid the survival of human beings. "If we don't protect wilderness today," Johnson continues, "we're not taking advantage of the potential that wilderness provides. It's a waste of an opportunity to establish a long-term investment in the region."

This particular region, Johnson reminds me, has a unique place in the history of the environmental movement. The original sponsor of the 1964 Wilderness Act was John Saylor, a Republican congressman from Johnstown, near Pittsburgh. Howard Zahniser, the author of the bill, grew up in Tionesta. Zahniser was Executive Director of the Wilderness Society and spent the last decade of his life working for passage of the Wilderness Act. Together, Saylor and Zahniser drafted the law creating wilderness areas "designated for preservation and protection in their natural condition" and requiring that the Secretary of

80

the Interior review roadless areas of federal lands eligible for wilderness protection every ten years, in order to provide "for the American people of present and future generations the benefits of an enduring resource of wilderness." Deciding against more wilderness areas in the very place Howard Zahniser made his home, say those who remember him, would be a sad denial of all he worked so hard to accomplish.

Old-growth forests also provide wildlife corridors, natural "highways" allowing plants and animals to move from one place to another so that they don't become isolated and vulnerable to extinction. Without these migration routes through old-growth forests, many species of songbirds may die out. As we walk back through the forest to the road, we hear some of those warblers making morning music in the trees. Johnson says that Scott Stoleson, an ornithologist with the Forest Service, is studying the relationship between cerulean warblers and white oak. For some reason, this species of warbler benefits in particular from old-growth white oak, a tree that is increasingly rare because of its great value to the timber industry.

"I'm worried about the beeches," Johnson says, looking around at the trees. I ask him how the hemlocks are doing. The hemlock woolly adelgid hasn't come here yet, he says. The cold winters here may be a barrier to the spread of that exotic pest, but according to the Forest Service the adelgid is less than a hundred miles away.

※

Monday morning turns cloudy and cool. Leaving Warren, I decide to drive out of town and go all the way to Heart's Content. Twenty acres of old-growth white pine and hemlock at Heart's Content was set aside by the Wheeler and Dusenbury Lumber Company over a hundred years ago and donated to the Forest Service in 1922. Since then Hearts Content has been one of the most studied old-growth sites in the country, and the Forest Service has acquired another hundred acres to add to the original preserve. The Civilian Conservation Corps constructed a campground, a picnic area, and pavilions in the 1930s; the campground provides access to the popular Hickory Creek Wilderness Trail, and a little further south, the Tanbark Trail hooks up with the North Country National Scenic Trail. There are also cross-country ski trails here along with a short trail that winds through the hemlock forest.

This too is an in-between place. Heart's Content lies directly between the Hickory Creek Wilderness Addition the Friends have proposed to the north, and the roadless Minister Valley area to the south. As a recreation area with cross-country ski trails and picnic grounds right off the road, along with a campground, Heart's Content offers a glimpse of the wild to the least rugged of visitors—like me—along with the prospect of a more rigorous experience for serious backpackers who can use it as a base camp for the Hickory Creek Hiking Trail. In the fall, small groups of college students come here on field trips to study the forest, but there are none of the tour buses or traffic jams found in so many national parks. The Friends of Allegheny Wilderness have suggested that Heart's Content be designated a National Recreation Area, where roads and camping facilities are allowed, but there are still opportunities for a wilderness experience.

I see half a dozen cars and trucks parked in the lot at the picnic grounds today, but the people who drove them here have all dispersed to the woods. I walk off alone down the scenic interpretive trail and into the hemlock woods. I'm wondering how the hemlock are doing here compared to other parts of the country.

These woods are drier and colder throughout the year than the ones I saw in the Smokies, so the moss is not as luxurious. I see dead trees, fallen trees, and piles of large woody debris among the living hemlocks, all signs of an old-growth forest left to its own devices. But there is also evidence of human stewardship. The Forest Service has constructed a number of deer fences, "exclosures" of posts and wire, making places the deer can't get into. Over the past twenty years, study plots here have yielded data disturbing to those who love the forest. In many plots, regrowth of vegetation is down by fifty percent. Until the deer herd can be thinned more drastically, these fences are one way of ensuring that the forest and its vegetation can regenerate.

The hemlock look fine; they are not as imposing as those in the Great Smoky Mountains, but hemlock grow in the shade of other trees, so their size can be deceptive. The long, frigid winters here have also disposed these trees to grow slowly, so while they may not be as big as the trees in the Smokies, some of them are actually hundreds of years old, and as Kirk Johnson said, cold winters have probably helped to prevent the spread of the hemlock woolly adelgid here, at least for the time being. The trail winds peacefully through green, fragrant woods; a cool breeze brushes the boughs of the hemlocks and sets them whispering amongst themselves. One other walker comes up behind me, clearing his throat. When I turn to look at the gray-bearded man wearing khaki pants, suspenders, a blue T-shirt, and a red visor cap, he apologizes. "I didn't want to startle you," he says politely. "I hope I'm not disturbing your solitary enjoyment of the woods." I assure him he is not, and he walks quietly on ahead of me, holding onto his wooden staff like a pilgrim and looking up at the trees.

The hemlock look fine, but the beech are another story. The beech that grow among the hemlock are succumbing to beech bark disease, a fungus that gets into the smooth, gray bark of the beech after the beech scale insect pierces it. Like so many other pests invading our native forests, beech scale came in with imported trees, arriving from Europe at the turn of the century and spreading throughout the Northeast, as far south as West Virginia. Beechnuts are an important food for many animals in the forest, including deer, bear, wild turkey, grouse, red foxes, squirrels, porcupines, chipmunks, and raccoons. They are also the preferred food for the larvae of the hairstreak butterfly, and the caterpillars of many other butterflies feed on the beech tree's leaves. Fewer beech trees mean another tear in the web of life that is a forest.

The loss of beech trees will also mean a less brilliant autumn; beech leaves turn bright gold in the fall. Old-timers have told me that autumn colors aren't as vivid these days as they used to be, and until now I've assumed their perception was due to a combination of aging eyes and nostalgia for bygone days. Now I see the elders may be on to something. As more and more hardwood trees succumb to blights and pests, the tapestry of autumn color fades. As global warming robs the cool temperatures of autumn nights, the process that creates the vibrant colors slows and dies. As proliferating deer destroy more and more tender young seedlings, the forest cannot be reborn. This is an in-between time in more ways than one. If we allow our forests to

83

shrink and our native trees to disappear, the glory of autumn colors may soon fade into the fabled past, a half-remembered time when the world was far more beautiful than now. I wonder how many of us would even know what we had lost.

CHAPTER SEVEN

Ode to Autumn

It starts in September with a bloom of rust on the hillside. First, the sumacs turning red, and then a few of the older maples. Soon, there is a smudging of orange as more of the maples turn. Then come the gold coins of the beech leaves, a rich yellow rain drenching the woods with color at moments when breezes stir the trees. In a few more days, the leaves of the stately white oak begin to turn maroon. Each day adds another dab, until the hillside is an artist's palette of color: amethyst, scarlet, saffron, cinnabar, topaz, bronze, and gold, all held up against the cerulean blue backdrop of the sky.

By November, the tamaracks are yellow candles burning against the faded sepia tones of the other barren trees. I wander into the woods, drawn by the newly open spaces under the trees, watching the light change, feeling the stress and strain of the past year drain away, like a long, deep sigh escaping from the ground beneath my feet.

In the Northeast deciduous forest, autumn is the time that everyone wants to be in the woods, or at least looking at them. "Leaf peepers" come from far away, like pilgrims, hoping to walk in the beauty of autumn color and be granted a moment of grace. Foresters, farmers, meteorologists, innkeepers, and general busybodies make their predictions for the "peak" days of color and speculate whether the season as a whole will be good, bad, or even—sometimes—spectacular.

Like sugaring season, the fall color season is a matter of timing, and in the end the timing may be known only to the trees. This much we know: as the hours of daylight diminish, one moment at a time, the process of photosynthesis slows, and with it goes the bright green pigment of chlorophyll. In the leaves of deciduous trees, the departure of chlorophyll exposes other pigments made of the sugars the tree has collected from sunlight: orange carotenoids and yellow xanthophylls. These pigments were there all along, but we can see them only when the chlorophyll is gone.

The brilliance of the fall display also depends on temperature. Warm September days favor the production of sugars containing the red pigment of anthocyanin in the leaves of maples and oaks. If warm days are followed by cool nights, this pigment stays in the leaves, ready to burst into flaming red.

As far as I'm concerned, there is no such thing as a "bad" fall color season, although sometimes rain and wind strip leaves from the trees before they have a chance to show off their autumn finery. Then the red and gold that might have been displayed on the trees is spread on the ground, and as I walk in the woods, I shuffle through rich piles of color and breathe in the scent of autumn exuded by the dying leaves. This is a scent no one can bottle, a perfume telling the story of love and loss and the passing of another year.

It's true that in years when sunny days provide optimum lighting the trees put on a better show. This year, rain comes up from the Gulf of Mexico, interrupting the performance, but by the time they get here, remnants of the hurricanes that devastated the Gulf Coast are little more than showers, and they make for morning fogs that mute the color on the hillsides to a soft, romantic blur. This is what John Keats called his "Season of mists and mellow fruitfulness/Close bosom-friend of the maturing sun." This is the time when hawthorn berries ripen, and hickory nuts fall from the trees with a startling thud. This is the time, as Emily Dickinson observed, that summer's garden flowers make a sudden exit:

> *The morns are meeker than they were*
> *The nuts are getting brown*
> *The berry's cheek is plumper*
> *The rose is out of town.*

Taking the place of the flowers are bins of rosy apples labeled Cortland, Crispin, Jonagold, and Northern Spy. There is no time of year when apples taste better, and at the farmers' market their fragrance scents the air with tart perfume for a few brief days. The sensual glory of autumn is a fleeting affair, made bittersweet because I know the long nights of winter are coming. It's time to take to the hills.

My own autumn odyssey leads me not to the leaf-peeper meccas of Vermont or New Hampshire, or even the Adirondacks, but to the place the Seneca called *Shegahunda*, the "vale of the three falls," in Letchworth State Park, only forty miles from my home. The park is a long finger following the Genesee River for seventeen miles as it cuts a deep gorge between the hills, a process that started eight thousand years ago at the end of the last ice age, and continues today. Along the way, the river tumbles over shelves of rock in three precipitous plunges, making the upper, middle, and lower falls. Ephemerals also spill down cliffs in run-offs whenever there has been sufficient rain. Viewing the autumn colors from lookouts stationed on the road that winds through the park is a favorite occupation here, and the waterfalls are lovely at any time of year. On an October day, I park my car in back of William Pryor Letchworth's home, now the Glen Iris Inn, and walk to the edge of his lawn for a view of the middle falls and the hillside beyond painted orange, yellow, and red by the autumn leaves. It's a popular spot for wedding photos, but on a weekday like today only a few tourists gather to aim their cameras at the falls. A golden light fills the gorge, and the waterfalls are roaring, fed by a week of rain. The air is frothy, and I walk along the trail beside the gorge until I see Letchworth's rainbow, a luminous arch of color in the mist.

A wealthy hardware merchant from Buffalo, Letchworth came to the Genesee Valley in 1858, looking for a summer home. Stepping off the train and standing on the trestle bridge high above the gorge, he saw a rainbow form in the mists over the falls, and thinking it an auspicious sign, he decided to buy the property and protect it from lumbering and industrial development. He converted the old tavern perched a few hundred yards away from the falls into his home, naming it "Glen Iris" for the goddess of the rainbow, messenger of the gods.   87

This is just one item from an extensive catalog of Letchworth lore. The tale of Mary Jemison, the "White Woman of the Genesee" who was captured by Shawnee warriors and eventually came to live here with the Seneca, has fascinated people around the world since a local doctor named James Seaver wrote down her story in 1823. His book, *The Life and Times of Mrs. Mary Jemison,* has been in print ever since. Letchworth brought Jemison's remains here to be buried on a hill behind the Glen Iris, and erected a statue to her memory.

The Seneca also tell the tale of Monashasha, a young mother who died here with her baby son. Her spirit lives on, they say, in the form of a white deer that roams the park.

"Once a long time ago," says the Seneca storyteller, "there was a hunter who lived in the great thunder of the Middle Fall. He was Joninedah, the Elk, and he and his wife, Monashasha, came with their son to live and hunt between the two great falls of the Genesee."

At first the small family was happy, but there came a time when Joninedah could find no game, and he grew despondent. Nothing Monashasha could say cheered her husband, and he began to speak of being cursed—even that she, Monashasha, was the source of his trouble. Joninedah's words made his wife so miserable that she began to believe what he said. There was only one way she could think of to remove the curse. And so, one night, as Joninedah lay sleeping, Monashasha took her little son and put off in their canoe into the river. As they approached the Middle Falls, she threw away the paddle, and they plunged into the roaring waterfall, her cry of despair echoing in the mist.

Hearing the cry in the night, Joninedah woke and went out to look for his wife and son. He searched for them in the darkness, with the sound of the thundering waterfall rushing in his ears. Just as dawn brought a ghostly gray light to the gorge, a white deer and its fawn appeared from the mist, stepping toward Joninedah and gazing at him with sad, accusing eyes.

"Then he knew," the storyteller says. "The white doe and her fawn were the spirits of his dead wife and son and they were asking him to join them. Slowly, no longer feeling the coldness of the morning, Joninedah walked to the brink of the fall and drew out his knife. Calling to his wife and child he plunged the knife into his chest and leaped into the churning waters far below to join his beloved Monanshasha."

I have not seen the white deer, but there is ghostly evidence of deer everywhere in the park. In some places the forest floor is eerily open under the trees, even in summer, as if a mower has been at work, cutting down the understory of saplings, shrubs, bushes, and wildflowers. This is not the work of mowers, but of a deer herd many people think is out of control. Joninedah would have no trouble hunting here today. An estimated one million deer now live in New York State, some thirty to thirty-five deer per square mile here in the southern tier, far above the carrying capacity of fifteen to twenty considered safe for the forest. In areas like Westchester County, where deer proliferate unchecked and feast on the easy pickings of suburban gardens, the number is sometimes reported to be as high as eighty deer per square mile.

Nationwide, the deer population has grown a hundred fold in the past century. At the beginning of the 1900s, agricultural clearing limited the animal's habitat, and unrestricted hunting reduced the number of deer in the country to about a half a million. Today there are reports of over twenty-five million deer in the United States. The fragmentation of forests and wilderness areas by commercial development favors deer, as they like the edges of woodlands more than the deep forest. We've got plenty of edges now. And in most places, predators like wolves, cougars, lynx, and bobcats are gone. The deer's main enemy is humans, but in New York State, hunting licenses are down by over thirteen percent, and the Department of Environmental Conservation is concerned that if the trend continues, the number of deer in New York will become increasingly unmanageable. Dedicated deer hunters are growing old and no longer devote the time they once did to roaming the woods in autumn, young people aren't attracted to the sport as they were in the past, preferring the sedentary indoor activity of computer games, and in some communities, people are opposed to the blood sport of hunting and killing deer.

Outdoor writer Ted Williams isn't one of them. "There's only one way to protect yourself, your family, and native ecosystems from the most dangerous and destructive wild animal in North America," he writes in the July/August 2005 issue of *Audubon*. You have to kill it with guns." Williams has called on environmentalists to join with hunters in addressing the problem of too many deer over-browsing our forests.

It's difficult for those who love the natural world and all its creatures to reconcile a reverence for life with hunting, but Williams and others like him say we have to recognize that too many deer are preventing the natural process of forest regeneration. All over the country, hungry deer devour the seedlings of native trees and shrubs, wipe out wildflowers, and destroy habitat for many songbirds as well as birds that nest on the ground. Nonlethal efforts such as deer contraception or fencing off areas to exclude the deer have proven neither cost-effective nor drastic enough to solve the problem. Even nature sanctuaries are allowing hunting on properties that would have once been off limits. Some suburban communities have hired sharpshooters to spend several days thinning the herd of does in places where deer proliferate. Ordinary hunters in search of the trophy buck with its rack of antlers don't always want to shoot does, and the truth is that hunters don't always want fewer deer. In states like Pennsylvania, "deer wars" have actually erupted between hunters and the game commission when it tried to issue more doe permits and reduce the deer herd's capacity to reproduce.

Here in Letchworth, at the Big Bend lookout, where I stop to look at the river cutting its path through the gorge, I count three does browsing peacefully under the trees near the parking lot, where hunters cannot come. Deer aren't quite as dumb as people think. They seem to know enough to avoid the places frequented by hunters, and one of the reasons some people believe more hunting should be allowed here is to convince the deer that this is not a refuge. Hunting permits are issued for the thirteen thousand acres outside the "safety zone" around the Glen Iris Inn, about twenty-two hundred permits annually. And a new state law has extended the hunting season this year to the weekend before Thanksgiving, in hopes of attracting more hunters to the woods. But in the "safety zone," the same one thousand acres of woodlands that William Pryor Letchworth tried to conserve, the problem of deer over-browsing the woods is particularly acute. In larger forests, like those in the Great Smoky Mountains, the deer can disperse and do less damage to native plants. If too many deer take refuge in smaller areas like this, the effect can be devastating. Letchworth knew the woodlands surrounding the vale of the three falls needed protection from the timber industry and the railroad. I doubt he could ever have imagined they would need protection from deer.

The browsing deer are lovely, with their long necks bent to the ground, the autumn sunlight glowing on their tawny fur, and once I would have thought them picturesque. Now they seem a menace. The truth is that the story of autumn is also the story of the hunt.

❧

On November 18th, the Friday afternoon before Thanksgiving, when I go to the grocery store to do my shopping, I am greeted by an unusual sight: men. Men in orange caps, men in camouflage, men in coveralls, men in jeans and boots, men in quilted vests. Old men, young men, short men, tall men, bearded men, and clean-shaven men. Men in pairs, and men alone. Pushing my shopping cart through the aisles, I peek at what all these men are putting in theirs. For the most part, no big surprises. Cold cuts, ground meat, bread, potato chips, milk, eggs, cereal, soda pop, beer. One man has a cart full of frozen pumpkin pies and Cool Whip. He must be in charge of dessert. As I pass by the checkout counters, I notice a slim young man standing in line and holding packages of celery, broccoli, and tofu. A vegan hunter?

"It's been busy all day," the cashier at the checkout says, to no one in particular. Men stream into the store, filling their carts with food and drink. They've come from out of town, drawn to the forests of the southern tier for the first day of shotgun season. Many are opening their hunting camps in the woods. Some are staying at motels, and some will be here all week to celebrate Thanksgiving with family and friends. For the past fifty years, New York's shotgun season has started on the first Monday after the fifteenth of November, and deer hunters have abandoned school or work to take to the woods. This year, the Department of Environmental Conservation is trying something new. Big game season will start tomorrow, on Saturday. Rifle hunting will also be allowed for the first time in Allegany and Cattaraugus counties. Teachers will probably be happy that high-school students won't have to pretend to be sick on Monday in order to hunt. Those who love forests hope the new laws will lure more hunters back to the sport and reduce the numbers of deer that are munching on the trees.

On Saturday morning, I drive to Letchworth again for a walk through the old-growth forest in the Dehgayasoh Valley led by Doug Bassett, the park's naturalist. Bassett is one of the treasures of the state park system. He has been roaming the woods here at Letchworth for over

91

thirty years, and he seems to know every inch of them. Since 1982, he has been leading tours of the biggest trees and the smallest bits of old-growth forest surviving in the park. He is as adept at communicating with five-year-olds as he is at speaking with senior citizens; I have heard him tailor his talks for either age group, depending on who shows up on a given Saturday morning. I have seen him crawl into the dark hollow at the base of a one-hundred-and-seventy-five-year-old ash tree, disappear inside the tree, then turn around and playfully poke out his head, like a leprechaun. I have watched him climb swiftly up a steep hillside, and after giving an informative talk on the hickory trees at the top, slide down the hill on his behind through piles of fallen leaves, because, he says, it's the quickest way back to the bottom of the hill. With the help of the other interpreters on the park staff, including Steph Spittal and Mary Underhill (who is no relation to the author), he puts out a quarterly booklet of information about the park called *The Genesee Naturalist*, illustrated with pen and ink drawings of owls, crows, mushrooms, and mice. For six dollars you can get your own subscription. Usually, the articles in the booklet discuss the flora and fauna currently living in the park, but the Winter 2005 issue featured a drawing of a mastodon to remind readers of the ice age origins of the Genesee Gorge. Farmers' plows have turned up the enormous skulls and tusks of mastodons that roamed here ten thousand years ago, and stone arrowheads with them, so we know that native people once hunted mastodons.

No one is certain why mastodons disappeared. When the climate warmed after the last ice age, conditions favoring these huge animals would have also changed, and the spruce-fir forests that they browsed retreated to higher elevations. It's thought that the mastodons, with their heavy, long fur and their layers of fat, couldn't adapt to the warmer climate. Now, as the climate warms to the hottest it's been in the past four hundred years, causing polar ice to melt and sea levels to rise, we may be witnessing unforeseen developments in the story of evolution. In 2004, a group of biologists from different countries around the world examined data on eleven hundred species of animals and plants to try to estimate their survival rate in the increasingly warmer climate of the twenty-first century. Their most conservative estimate, published in the journal *Nature*, concluded that fifteen percent of these animals and plants would disappear by the year 2050 as a result of global warming alone. Ironically, the proliferation of one species—the deer—is responsible for destroying some of the precious habitat for those that remain.

As I wait for Bassett in the parking lot of the visitors' center, along with a van full of Boy Scouts from Rochester and two bird watchers toting cameras and binoculars, I listen to crows and blue jays calling in the woods. Then I hear gunshots. We are still in the "safety zone" of one thousand acres surrounding the Glen Iris Inn, but obviously the hunters aren't far away. The air is fresh and cool, the fragrance of fallen leaves muted by the freezing temperatures of the past few days. A thin white layer of snow glazes the ground, but the sun is out, and I have a feeling the snow won't last for long.

It doesn't take long for Doug Bassett to appear, hands in the pockets of his insulated blue coveralls. The scouts pile into their van and I hop into the truck with Bassett along with the bird watchers. As he drives down the road leading from the visitors' center to the Dehgayasoh Woods, he talks about the deer problem, and he tells us that thirty years ago, when he first began studying the flora and fauna of the park, there were thirteen different kinds of orchids growing here; now there are none. The trillium are also gone, he says. Deer candy. A life-long hunter himself, he acknowledges that there is no easy way to hunt deer in the safety zone, given how many people congregate here, including park workers. In winter, when skiing and snowmobiles are popular forms of recreation for visitors to the park, the dangers of bullets hitting an unsuspecting tourist are still a worry, and adjacent landowners are concerned that allowing more hunting here could allow more men with guns to stray onto their property. The money necessary for studying the issue, gathering data, and making recommendations about managing the deer isn't there, much less the money for implementing possible solutions such as an effective means of birth control for deer, and as Bassett often points out when talking about the dangers to forests here and elsewhere around the country, "there's no superfund for trees."

93

The woods we are here to see are at the end of a road, beyond a chalet and a pair of cabins perched on the edge of a ridge. As we gather around him, Bassett says these woods have never known a farmer's plow. Ten thousand years ago, the ground we are standing on was covered in mile-high sheets of ice. Deer will lead the way for us into the woods called Dehgayasoh, for there are no trails marked here, only deer paths to follow down the hill. Dehgayasoh, he tells us, is a Seneca word meaning "many nameless spirits." Many creatures we can name live in these woods today, and before we start down the hill towards the creek that we will cross to reach a hemlock forest on the other side, Bassett points out the tracks of gray squirrels and deer mice leaving the signs of their story in the snow. We hear crows and blue jays, and we see juncos and a woodpecker in the trees, all winter birds that will stay until spring. A red-tailed hawk soars overhead, and then we see the long, dark shape of a turkey vulture gliding towards the gorge, less than a mile away. From where we stand, we can still hear the roaring music of the falls.

Following the deer paths into the woods, we see a variety of very old hardwood trees casting long shadows on the snow. Thousands of years ago, Bassett tells us, birds and squirrels brought the first seeds and nuts of trees from the refuges of the southern Appalachians to repopulate this forest after the glaciers withdrew. As we walk through the woods, Bassett points out white oak and black oak, big-toothed aspen, and tulip tree, prized for the long, straight grain of its wood. Its distinctive four-lobed leaves lie around it on the ground. This is the tree chosen by Edgar Allen Poe to guard the buried treasure of a pirate in his story "The Gold Bug." The tulip tree grows straight and tall with few lower branches, making it difficult for the characters in the story to climb. Poe must have known his trees. The trunk of a mature tulip tree can be free of lower branches for as high as eighty feet. Donald Peattie calls it "the king of the Magnolia family, the tallest hardwood tree in North America." Also known as yellow poplar (although it is not a true poplar), the swiftly growing tree can reach heights of two hundred feet in the southern Appalachians, where it doesn't face our long, hard winters.

We also see ancient white pine, and valuable specimens of white oak and black cherry. What these woods don't have, Bassett says to the Boy Scouts, are any "baby trees" to replace the older trees that fall. For understory, there is only Chinese barberry, a prickly, non-native shrub the deer won't eat. Barberry has become a favorite for suburban landscaping precisely because it survives where deer are a problem; now it has escaped to the woods. Invasive species like barberry can take over where native plants are not allowed to regenerate. It's a more subtle process than a mile-high sheet of ice, but in its way it's just as destructive to the character of the woods.

Bassett likes to read history in trees. He points to the broken, clawed shapes of the tops of white pine trees, evidence of an ice storm or a wind storm here in the 1920s.

One of the tallest pine trees is dead—still standing, skeletal. Other trees have fallen. We look at the jagged stump of an oak tree and the long trunk lying beside it on the ground. The stump itself is nearly six feet tall. It is splintered and bent, but the jagged edges of wood are painted white with snow, and rich green moss is growing at its base. No longer alive itself, the tree is still supporting life. This is the kind of death I have always admired. In a forest, nothing is wasted, nothing is useless, and as long as seedlings and saplings grow up to replace the older trees, nothing is really dead. Even as the fallen tree decays, the essence of life remains. The form of the tree breaks down and gives shape instead to the ground, the birds, the insects, the mice. Maybe this is what the Seneca meant by the "many nameless spirits" here, the coming and going of life in all its manifestations: light and water, feather and stone, leaf and bark, flesh and bone.

As we thread our way single file down a long, narrow deer path we hear the insistent music of Dehgayasoh Creek. Beyond the creek, in the shadow of the ridge behind us, grows an evergreen forest of hemlock. We pick our way across a shallow spot in the creek, using cold, wet rocks as stepping stones, and then we climb up the bank and into the hemlock woods, where we stop to take our lunch. The hemlock woods are cool in the shade of the hill we have just descended, but the sun has climbed over the ridgeline, high enough to send a few warm shafts of sunlight through the trees. I think the hemlock must like to stand on a slope like this, so close to the sound of water. Some of them lean towards the creek, as if they are listening to water music playing on the stones. The trees do not fear the coming of winter, or the coming of night. They grow slowly, they grow in the shadows, they grow in tune with the many nameless spirits of the woods. These trees are old enough to have survived the deer that like to munch on the soft green tips of young saplings. But I don't see any young saplings coming up among the tall old trees. If deer continue to prevent the process of regeneration, the woods we are seeing today will no longer exist a hundred years from now.

After we've all had a bite to eat, we cross back over the creek and head up the hill towards the road, following Doug Bassett as he cuts a diagonal path through the trees. I am glad these woods still exist today, and glad that I can walk them. I am glad for the walking stick Bill bought me at a hiking store in Tennessee to steady me on the slope where the ground is slick with snowmelt. I am glad for my feet, my ankles, my knees, my muscles moving me up the hill, glad for my heart that is pumping blood to my muscles, glad for the sun that is warming my face. "Walk and touch peace every moment," says Thich Nhat Hanh. "The path is you."

> *That is why it will never tire of waiting.*
> *Whether it is covered with red dust,*
> *Autumn leaves,*
>   *Or icy snow. . .*

Some of the Boy Scouts opt for charging straight up the steepest slope instead of taking the longer diagonal way. They arrive after the rest of us, breathless and rosy-cheeked and a little muddy from taking falls as they scrambled up the hill. As we gather once more to look around us, we see a flash of wings in the trees. It's a yellow-bellied sapsucker, a bird that should have left the woods to fly south by now.

Before we leave, Bassett reminds us that there are stories here we can never know. The glaciers that shaped this valley wiped out all evidence of people who might have lived here once, before the ice age. These, too, are the "many nameless spirits" of the woods.

Prompted by the grown-ups, the Boy Scouts offer their thanks to Bassett, and he smiles and nods. The boys pile into the van with their leaders, while the bird watchers and I get back into the truck with Bassett. As we pass the chalet by the side of the road, we see a deer carcass hanging from a tree. "There's someone who got their deer today," says one of the bird watchers sitting behind me in the truck. It's a doe, one that will not be giving birth next spring, a sacrifice to the nameless spirits of the Dehgayasoh Woods. I do not know if killing the doe will help keep the Dehgayasoh Woods alive. But today, at least, I think, it couldn't hurt.

CHAPTER EIGHT
Rainforest

Think of all the words we have to describe the color green: emerald, jade, celadon, chartreuse, teal, leaf, lime, olive, sage, mint, verdure, verdigris, pine, spring. Think of the dark splendor of spruce, the pale frothing of fern, the wet mystery of moss. All of these shades of green are here in Washington State's Olympic National Forest, one of the few temperate rainforests on the planet. On average, a hundred and forty inches of rain fall in the valleys of the Olympic Forest each year. That's about twelve feet of rain, making this one of the greenest places I have ever seen.

Most of the rain comes in January and February. June is considered the dry season. Yet when Bill and I arrive at Lake Quinault in mid June, the rain seems to start every ten minutes, a quiet drizzle that gives way to sunshine for another ten minutes before the rain begins again. When it is not raining, a ragged white shawl of mist cloaks the hills around the lake. The result is a gentle jungle, one without poisonous snakes, chattering monkeys, or crocodiles. What this rainforest has is the perfect environment for evergreen trees.

Glaciers sculpted the valleys here during the last ice age. Pollen records show that conifers began to grow a few thousand years later, and have been here ever since: Sitka spruce, with its strong but light-weight wood, Douglas fir, with its straight, tall trunk, shade-loving western hemlock, growing beneath the other trees, and rot-resistant red cedar, the tree indigenous people used for making their canoes. Conifers are ideally suited for this environment, their pointed tops reaching to the sky for any available sunlight, their wood and their evergreen needles storing water all year round. On the Olympic Peninsula, where winds from the south bring warm, moist air off the

Pacific to condense into rain as the air climbs towards the coastal mountain ranges, conifers outnumber deciduous trees a thousand to one. In winter, the temperature rarely drops below freezing, and in summer, it rarely surpasses eighty degrees Fahrenheit. In these conditions, trees grow fast, sometimes as much as two to three feet a year. So although ninety-seven percent of the old-growth evergreen forest here was ravaged, much of it during the great clear-cut era of the early twentieth century—and at the Lake Quinault Lodge there are old sepia-toned photographs of the naked hills to prove it—the enormous trees here seem more than a mere hundred years of age. Among them are a few giants that survived the clear cutting. The Quinault Valley has six champion evergreens, including the largest Sitka spruce and the largest western red cedar in the world, both trees that are over a thousand years old. Conifers like these are the original trees; three hundred million years ago, before the evolution of flowering plants, all of Earth's forests were evergreen forests. So coming here gives me a glimpse of what a truly ancient forest might have been like.

The moment Bill and I set foot on the trail across from the ranger station on the south side of Lake Quinault, I give myself over to green. The evergreen trees rise all around me, a polyphonic symphony of green. Their bark, covered in emerald mosses, is as green as their needles, their branches dripping with the long green hair of hanging moss. High up on the trees are pale green licorice ferns, plants growing on plants where crevices hold just enough soil to root them. In the understory, sword ferns grow three feet high, and beneath them, carpets of oxalis, with clusters of leaves that look like giant clover. Graceful maidenhair ferns grow at the bases of trees, and hugging the ground are the starry green leaves of sweet woodruff. Here and there are bits of white and red: foam flowers lift stalks of tiny white petals against the green of the ferns, bunchberry dogwood, called "false dogwood" because its flowers with their four flat, white petals resemble those of the tree that we know in the east; bleeding heart, with its small drops of red; and in between the ground and the trees is salmonberry with large, raspberry-shaped fruit drooping from its green cane.

Water is in the berry, the cane, the stem, the root. Water is in my skin, my hair, my eyes, my hands. Water is what connects me to the web of life, where everything is connected. Without water, without rain, without mud and mist and river and lake, nothing of what we call life on earth could exist. I am always swimming in the sea of life. It's no wonder walking in the rainforest makes me feel at home.

A gentle rain begins as we walk along on the Quinault Loop Trail, and I pull the hood of my jacket over my head. Normally rainy days make me grumpy, but here the rain is so benign and the trees and ferns and mosses so lush that my immediate response is a feeling of delight. The temperature is in the mid sixties, and the air feels soft and wet on my face and hands, with the quiet patter of raindrops providing background music. In a few minutes, the rain stops, the sun comes out again, and everything gleams. Walking here is like traversing one of the enchanted realms of a children's story, a place where fairies and leprechauns might live beneath the ferns and hobbits make homes in the hollow trunks of trees. The presence of so much green seems to stimulate the imagination; it is also reassuring. Green is the color we live by, the color of health and prosperity, the color of youth and hope, the color of healing. In such a green and hopeful world, it's impossible not to be at ease.

So far, Bill and I have been alone on the trail, but as we turn to climb the hill we hear someone else behind us—a man running with his two dogs. We step aside to let them pass and murmur a greeting. The runner nods and keeps his pace as he jogs past us, breathing heavily, his legs pumping. The dogs pant, running behind him, and they all disappear up the trail. It looks like a good workout, but I don't want to hurry. I'd rather stroll and enjoy the lush green dream of the rainforest creating calm in my heart and mind and spreading a sense of relaxed well-being throughout my body. As I breathe in the humid air, I am breathing peace. I'm in the Garden of Eden, the primordial homestead, before the fall from grace. There's nothing chasing me, *101* and there's no need to run.

The conditions for a temperate rainforest like this one exist in only a few other places: Australia, New Zealand, Chile, and small areas along the coasts of Norway, Great Britain, and Japan. Two thirds of all the temperate rainforest in the world is right here, on the western edge of North America, in a narrow, comma-shaped band extending for twelve hundred miles along the coast from Alaska to the Olympic peninsula. Evergreen trees often grow right down to the sea, and while many of them are still being cut, some, like all of those in Olympic National Park and many here in the Olympic National Forest, are off-limits to logging now. Invasive insects don't bother the trees here much, either. The western hemlock, for instance, because it originated in Asia, is immune to the woolly hemlock adelgid that is decimating trees in the east.

Windthrow, however, is another matter. As Bill and I walk up the Quinault Loop Trail, we see evidence of the storm that hit on February fourth this year—trees that are bent, off-kilter, or on the ground. One lies strewn beside the trail in bits, shattered to pieces by wind. Killer storms regularly batter the Olympic Peninsula—-on average once every ten years. But just as hurricanes are increasing in the Gulf of Mexico, they are developing here more often as well. In the past seven years, the Olympic Peninsula has already seen three major storms. Scientists blame global climate change, and if there are still skeptics in other parts of the country, climate change is taken seriously in the Pacific Northwest. In a climate like this one, which is already fairly warm, even a small increase in temperature could create what the Puget Sound Action Team has called "a slow-motion natural disaster." Over the sixty years prior to 2008, snowpack in the Cascades declined by thirty percent, so there was far less water melting into rivers and streams. If the trend continues, there are bound to be serious problems for hydroelectric power, agriculture, and tourism. With three such important elements of the Northwest economy in danger, elected officials here have taken the lead in making changes they hope will mitigate some of the impact of climate change. Seattle mayor Greg Nickels is urging other cities around the nation to join him in signing the Mayors Climate Protection Agreement, which commits to the Kyoto Protocol standards for reducing greenhouse gas emissions, something our federal government has failed to do. Oregon governor Ted Kulongoski has demanded tougher emission standards for new cars and trucks. Seattle and Portland are both building light rail systems and bike paths and buying hybrid-electric vehicles for city government employees. Still, it doesn't look as if the American love affair with the automobile is going to end any time soon. The traffic around both cities is some of the worst I have ever seen.

Americans are victims of our own affluence, with our automobiles, our appliances, and the garbage we produce from the many products we buy and throw away. The typical American produces some fifteen thousand pounds of carbon dioxide a year, the highest per capita amount in the world. Here in the Northwest, the prospect of losing the battle against climate change is no longer talked about as "if" but as "when," and "when" may come much sooner than most of us realize. Some experts say that in ten years or less, we will reach the tipping point when the damage to our atmosphere and our climate becomes irreversible.

Trees can help. All plants take carbon dioxide from the air and use it to fuel their growth. Trees, because they produce wood that accumulates as they grow, are particularly effective at storing carbon, sometimes for hundreds of years. The carbon goes into the tree instead of warming the atmosphere. Cutting down trees contributes to the problem of climate change as much as driving too many automobiles that only get ten miles to the gallon. Planting trees can offset some of our carbon emissions, but not all. A mature tree absorbs thirteen pounds of carbon dioxide a year. So the average American, with fifteen thousand pounds of CO_2 emissions, needs over a thousand mature trees to offset what he or she alone produces each year. The truth is that to combat climate change, we must both reduce our carbon emissions *and* protect forests like this one. "When forests are conserved and sustainably managed," the Pacific Forest Trust maintains, "they absorb and hold immense amounts of carbon dioxide, mitigating global warming." And while tree planting can help, conserving mature forests is "even more important."

Proponents of logging like to emphasize the benefits to local economies, undeniably important to the people who live here. Not only jobs are at stake; on federally owned lands a percentage of profits on the timber cut is paid to the local communities, helping to fund libraries and keep property taxes down. But when those in the timber industry use the term "healthy forests," it is important to understand that they mean "productive forests." Compared to the selective cutting of a few trees, clear cutting of large stands of trees, especially with today's machinery, is fast and efficient, and opens the forest to sunlight, allowing for quick regeneration of another crop of trees to be cut again forty or fifty years later, as soon as the trees are big enough to be profitable. The clear-cut area may be replanted—usually with whatever type of tree is considered the most valuable in the marketplace. The result will be an even-aged stand of trees, sometimes a monoculture with none of the rich tapestry of life one sees in a forest left to its own devices. In the meantime, habitat for some species will have been destroyed, the monoculture of new trees invites dangerous pests as if to a banquet laid out free for the taking, the opportunity for human beings to know the forest is gone, and so is the cooling effect an older forest has on the atmosphere. If done carelessly, clear cutting also results in erosion and contributes to flooding.

As we traveled Highway 101 to Quinault Lake, we saw numerous clear cuts where no attempt had been made to leave even a narrow "beauty bar" of trees along the road to disguise the destruction. Many of the cuts were of the so-called "dirty clear-cut" variety, where some of the debris from the logged trees is left in piles instead of being hauled away or burned. This technique is intended to mimic the effects of a natural wind storm, leaving some woody debris to provide habitat for wildlife, and protecting the ground—except that the largest trees are gone, unable to act as nurses for new seedlings or to return nutrients to the soil. Foresters hope that, compared to traditional clear cuts, the dirty clear cuts will create more natural and diverse new stands of trees, at least in places that are not cut again, and in any event it will take fifty to seventy-five years to know for sure. In the meantime, the effect on the eyes and the soul remains distressing. Once you have seen the ragged stumps and rutted soil left behind on a clear cut, you have little appetite for lumber. The dirty clear cut may be only the lesser of two evils.

104

Clear cutting around the Olympic National Forest has also been a factor in allowing wind to damage trees. On the southwest end of Lake Quinault, where the forest faces the coast, clear cutting on tribal lands beyond the boundary of the national forest has opened a corridor for wind. With the tallest trees gone, there is no longer a barrier to the storms that blow in off the Pacific Ocean. William Clark of the Lewis and Clark Expedition preferred to call the Pacific the "Great Western Ocean," since, as he wryly observed, he had found it anything but peaceful. Looking for a winter camp along the mouth of the Columbia River in November 1805, he wrote "the swells continued high all the evening and we are compelled to form an Encampment on a Point scarcely room sufficient for us all to lie cleare of the tide water . . . we are all wet and disagreeable, as we have been for several days."

Some windthrow from the storms that batter the "Pacific" coast is both natural and inevitable, part of the cycle of life and death in any forest. Fallen trees provide openings in the forest canopy where new young trees can find sunlight and grow. Fallen trees also act as nurses to seedlings. On our walks through the rainforest, we see colonnades of trees that have grown up along a nurse, seeding themselves on the fallen log where fertile debris has collected. The new trees send roots down around the sides of the log, and when the log rots away, it leaves a row of trees looking as if they are standing on stilts. The fallen nurse logs that create these trees are a natural part of the life cycle in the unique environment of the rainforest. So are the storms.

But since the time of Lewis and Clark, climate change has created an even less "pacific" ocean than the one that William Clark found on his winter encampment. Climate scientists say that greenhouse gases trapping heat in the oceans cause more intense storms, like those that devastated the Gulf Coast in recent years, and the one that hit the coast of the Pacific Northwest in February 2008, causing unnatural levels of destruction.

The evidence is all around us on the Quinault Loop Trail. As we walk the trail, we pass many fallen trees that have been sectioned to keep the way clear. The wood of the fast-growing evergreen trees is dense and strong, but their roots are often shallow, making them vulnerable to wind. Bill begins photographing the round cross-sections, examining the different shapes and colors of the wood and their annual rings. Some of the cuts are very fresh, from trees that fell in the February storm and were only recently cut to clear the trail. Others are older, displaying wood that is aged and covered with moss and lichen.

It's not just the fallen trees that are covered with green mosses. Each living branch is shaggy with green. Entire trees are covered in moss, so it is often difficult to tell one type of tree from another. When I stroke the moss growing on one of the fallen trees, it is soft and moist on my fingertips. I can feel the miniscule forest of tiny, fine hairs on the stems of the moss that collect moisture and store it for this plant that has no roots, no flowers, and no seeds. As we walk through the forest, moss collects on my boots, and I find strands of it in my hair. I think if I stayed here long enough the moss would grow on me. Mosses are opportunists. They will grow almost anywhere. In the east, moss will often grow on the cool, northern-facing side of a tree, so in a dense forest you can sometimes tell what direction you're going in by watching where the moss appears. Here, in the temperate rainforest, that would be impossible. The moss is everywhere.

The soft green mosses are beautiful, and they give this environment its unusual appearance, but mosses are also another link in the web of life that makes the rainforest such an extraordinary environment. Mosses help to collect the abundant rainwater from torrential storms, reducing flooding. They hold the water and make it available later, during periods of drought. They offer nesting materials to birds. Mosses, with no root systems, take all their nutrients from the atmosphere. In the process, they bring nitrogen from the air into the soil when they decay.

The moss-covered trees make the rainforest a unique visual experience, but what drew the timber industry here was the enormous trees themselves. Most of them are gone; we see their stumps along the trail, some still bearing the spring holes cut to hold boards where lumberjacks would stand, six feet up on either side of the tree, holding a saw between them and pushing it back and forth until they could make the cuts they needed to fell the giant trees. The stumps are ghostly reminders of what this forest must have looked like a hundred years ago.

Just a mile from the ranger station on the South Shore road, however, the world's largest Sitka spruce still grows, a short stroll in from the road, at the edge of a field not far from the lake. The next morning we go to see it. Fifty-five feet and seven inches in circumference, its base sprawls around it like knobby foothills. It towers to one hundred and ninety-one feet high, more like a mountain peak than a tree. Its purplish bark is scaley. Perhaps it survived the logging crews because it was already too big to be cut.

Or perhaps this tree has a particularly powerful and long-lived hamadryad, the type of nymph that the ancient Greeks believed inhabited a tree and personified its life spirit. Once, we worshipped trees like this one as sacred, and respected the spirits that lived in them. Destroying the tree and its spirit risked the wrath of the gods. Such myths embodied a simple truth that modern people, who rely on science to explain the natural world, seem to forget—without forests, civilization as we know it cannot exist. A thing is sacred if it is essential, and without the myths and rituals that once defined what is essential, says Karen Armstrong in her book *A Short History of Myth*, the sacred dies. Perhaps it is because we have lost that long-term sense of what is sacred that we have allowed our forests to be destroyed for short-term profits.

Today, plenty of Sitka spruce are cut regularly, here on the Olympic peninsula, and in Canada. They are the largest of all spruce, and they grow only in North America. The strength-to-weight ratio of Sitka spruce is unmatched by any other timber, meaning that no other wood is so light and at the same time so strong. This unique quality made Sitka spruce ideal for the early aircraft industry, but it is also favored for the soundboards of pianos, violins, and guitars because its clear, straight grain produces a uniform tone. Each type of wood, and even each tree, depending on its age and size and shape, has a different molecular structure, and each type of wood, combined with other woods in an instrument, vibrates in a different way and produces a different kind of sound. Makers of the steel-string guitars used to play folk music like the light, straight-grained spruce for the front of 107 their instruments, and a heavier wood like rosewood for the backs. This combination allows for a deeper, more complex sound than one type of wood alone would make. Compared to Engelmann spruce or European spruce, Sitka spruce soundboards produce a clean, bright sound that blue-grass musicians especially like for showcasing their finger picking. For strumming, the warm, mellow tone made by an old-growth Adirondack spruce soundboard is unmatched, but this wood is now so rare that it can be found only on vintage guitars that can sometimes be worth thousands of dollars. Destruction of old-growth trees has done damage over the years not just to our forests, not just to our climate, but even to our music. Finding the wood to make superior instruments is becoming increasingly more difficult, and if the guitars, violins, and pianos of yesteryear sound better than those made today, it's not always the workmanship, but sometimes the wood itself that was superior.

Evergreens dominate the rainforest, and the most common deciduous tree here is a puzzle to us at first. It resembles the paper birch we see back east, with white bark mottled black, like a page scribbled on by a sloppy scribe leaving blotches of ink. After consulting the pocket guide to western trees I bought at the ranger station, we determine that the tree we're seeing everywhere by the side of the road isn't birch, but red alder, named for the red heartwood under the bark. Indigenous people used the tree to make a red dye—for baskets, for fish nets (the red dye made the nets invisible in the water), and even for skin paint. Alder also makes excellent firewood, and it has been used for centuries here to make fires for smoking the region's once abundant wild salmon.

On the outside, the alder's bark isn't naturally white; it becomes so because of an artful lichen that grows on the tree bark, painting it white and black. Like the red wood within the tree, the alder's root system is unseen, but it provides another important service. In a symbiotic relationship with the tree, a bacterium named *frackia* lives in nodules on the alder's roots, fixing nitrogen from the atmosphere to be stored in the soil, making it fertile for other trees. Alder likes to invade slopes where other trees have been cut. Growing quickly, it holds the ground, enriches it with nitrogen, and shelters it while evergreens take hold. This is an example of cooperation and interdependency that I see only infrequently among human beings. We could study forests, I think, not just to observe how trees grow, but how they grow together, utilizing each other's unique talents and abilities. Maybe we human beings could learn to do the same.

Like the red alder, the red cedar trees also have a unique appearance. Red cedar is easy to spot because it is the one tree that doesn't gather emerald mosses as most of the other trees in the rainforest do. Its bark is too acidic. Cedar is uniquely rot-resistant, making it perfect for the beautiful dugout canoes the Quinault people made. As the trees age, the trunks become fluted and the bark becomes gray, the color of old silver. I picture them as the first columns in the first temples, the sacred groves where people first worshipped the mysteries of the universe. In the Middle East, where the famous cedars of Lebanon were thought to be the home of the gods, cedar wood was specified for building sanctuaries. In modern times Canadian artist Emily Carr, who painted the red cedar grove that once stood in Vancouver's Stanley Park, said "God's too big to be squeezed into a stuffy church, but I feel Him there in the spaces between the trees."

Here on the Olympic Peninsula many of the largest red cedar trees have been cut down and made into shingles. Today, the labor involved in felling such trees just to chop them up into shingles strikes me as ludicrous. But I know that the Arts and Crafts style houses built for the well-to-do all over the West in the early twentieth century are covered with these cedar shingles, as is the Lake Quinault Lodge. Our own house back east, built in 1971, is sided with cedar planks, and even in our damp climate, cedar is the one type of lumber used in the original construction of the house that shows not a bit of rot over thirty years later. Cedar wood also has its own natural property of insulation, keeping our house pleasantly cool in the summer and comfortably warm in the winter, saving on energy—and carbon emissions—in the process. When our house was built by the original owner, the cedar wood was already expensive. Most of the highest-quality old-growth red cedar in the United States has been logged off, and most of it was never even replanted. Now it is so rare that it is outrageously expensive; many home builders won't even consider using it for construction today. But it is still popular for hot tubs, garden furniture, and decks. And red cedar is still being cut in British Columbia—over cut, some say, meaning that logging companies are not leaving enough of the younger trees to sustain regeneration.

It's no wonder there are few large cedar trees left. But at the top of the appropriately named Big Cedar Trail on the northern side of Quinault Lake is the world's largest western red cedar. We arrive at the trailhead in a steady rain, so we sit for a while and eat our lunch in the car, waiting for the sun, which is sure to come out again in a few minutes. When it does, we walk past a field of purple foxglove, dripping wet and sparkling in the sunshine, and make our way into the rainforest. The trail leads steadily uphill, part of it on a wooden staircase built against the slope, and then on a narrow, muddy path that winds through the enormous roots of the hemlocks gripping the hillside.

As we scramble up the final, steep ascent to the top of the hill we meet a man and woman coming down, carrying binoculars. "You're in for a treat," the woman says, as we step aside to let her pass. "There's a pileated woodpecker at the very top of the big cedar." The woodpecker is gone by the time we get there. But I can see why the bird would be attracted to this skyscraper of a tree. Sixty-three and a half feet in circumference and one hundred seventy-four feet tall, the cedar tree is like a ruined tower rising above us, half-dead and hollow inside, its top broken off, a few branches still bearing green needles. It must have survived at the top of this ridge where it has stood for a thousand years because there was no easy way to fell it here, no space to allow for it to be cut up and carried away. Perhaps, like the Sitka spruce, this tree also has a particularly powerful and long-lived hamadryad to protect it.

It's raining again, and I can't resist the urge to go inside. Hollow trees like this one provided temporary homes for the earliest settlers to the region, sanctuaries in which to escape the elements. When I climb over the tree's two-foot-high sill of jagged wood at the base, I am in a kind of one-room cabin about twenty feet across. Immediately, I feel the same protective and tempering effect of the cedar wood that I have in my cedar-clad home back east. The air inside the hollow tree is pleasantly warmer and dryer than that outside, and faintly aromatic. The Quinault people called the red cedar the tree of life because it contributed to so many aspects of their survival that it was indispensable. The cedar tree gave them boards for longhouses, bark for baskets, and enormous, waterproof logs for dugout canoes. The Quinault even took the soft inner bark of the cedar and pounded it into a kind of fabric they used to make waterproof capes and helmets, items I think would come in very handy in this climate. Further up the coast, in Alaska, indigenous

110

people used the tall cedar with its soft, easily carved and painted wood for their storied totem poles.

This tree, already hollow all the way to the top, has been carved, by age, to resemble an enormous telescope pointing towards the sky. Looking up, I glimpse a wedge of daylight high above me. Looking around, I see the ruddy wood of the cedar hanging in ragged curtains. Looking out through the narrow "door" on the other side of the tree, I see the green world of the rainforest, where water drips from every leaf and stem, ferns cover the ground, mosses cover the trees, and the trees grow silently in the rain.

Trees like this one allow me to imagine—and mourn—the forest that existed here before the modern era, a forest of many enormous red cedar, home to the gods. The fact that the ancient forests of the Pacific Northwest still exist in any form at all may be thanks to a creature most people have never seen—the northern spotted owl.

CHAPTER NINE
Owl Prowl

Owls have always invoked power, wisdom, insight, and magic. Nocturnal creatures of the forest with the ability to see in the dark, owls are portrayed as partners to the supernatural world. The sorcerer Merlin travels with an owl on his shoulder, and the young wizard Harry Potter has an owl to deliver his mail. Symbol of Athena, the Greek goddess of wisdom, the owl is a companion to scholars, poets, and philosophers, leading them to knowledge of the unseen, the world of the imagination, and the dark realm of dreams.

Guardians of the night, owls are often associated with death, but these birds of prey actually signal a forest's vitality. "As top predators with large home ranges," says Dr. Jim Duncan, an ornithologist specializing in owls, "many owls are good indicators of healthy ecosystems and sustainable development." Without abundant prey and plentiful trees to provide shelter and nesting spots, in other words, owls will disappear. A forest without owls might be a forest in trouble.

There are good reasons to admire owls. Owls have excellent sight and extraordinary hearing. An owl's eyes are like binoculars, with the ability to judge depth and distance as they hunt. Owls can also dilate their pupils the entire width of their eyes to take in maximum light. The owl's retina contains more of the rod-shaped cells that gather any and all available light, giving it an advantage over other creatures when evening shadows fall. When I am out in the woods at night, I quickly lose my bearings, and I often lose my nerve. Trees close in around me and block out the light. I feel as if I have fallen into a void. What are all those rustling sounds? Blind in the encroaching darkness, I find my hearing amplified. I detect the scurrying feet of nocturnal creatures going abroad, easily finding their way, sometimes just by using a highly developed sense of smell that I can only guess at, along with a keen awareness of the placement of every rock and every tree. I want my flashlight, but when I turn it on it illuminates only a few yards ahead of me. In the end I walk as quickly as possible back to camp and the comforting sight of a lantern chasing away the darkness. Out in the country at night, I am truly at ease only when the moon is full, flooding the sky with light. But in places where I can find no light, the owl is right at home.

Owls actually prefer the darkness that I have learned to fear. The owl's extraordinary hearing gives it another advantage after dark. Owls have the power to pinpoint prey just by listening for the faint sound of dry leaves rustling on the ground as a mouse scurries through the forest. Studies have shown they can do it blindfolded. Their soft, velvety feathers may make owls seem cuddly, but this too is an adaptation improving their prowess as nocturnal hunters. The tips of an owl's feathers are serrated, allowing it to stroke the air noiselessly as it flies. Soft, noiseless feathers enable owls to swoop silently towards their prey—they are the stealth bombers of the bird world. Their somber gray and brown plumage helps to conceal them both at night, when they blend into the darkness, and during the day, when they roost wedged tightly against the bark of a tree or in the eaves of a barn.

All in all, the owl is a creature of power and mystery. The Chinese philosopher Lao Tzu might have been speaking of the owl when he said:

> *Seeing into darkness is clarity*
> *Knowing how to yield is strength*
> *Use your own light*
> *And return to the source of light.*
> *This is called practicing eternity.*

114

Gliding silently over an open field at dusk, an owl can spot a rabbit moving in the grass, and swoop down to capture it. With its strong legs and sharp talons, an owl can carry off creatures two or three times its own size. Hawks have the same abilities; hawks and owls often share the same territory, the hawk hunting by day, and the owl by night. Owls will even occupy nests made by hawks. We understand that hawks are predators, but we still tend to think of owls as companions. With their large-looking heads and blinking, wide-eyed stares, owls resemble humans to the extent that we identify with them and even emulate them with big round glasses to magnify our own poor sight. Owls have also adapted to human society, surviving long, cold northern winters by roosting in barns and feeding on the mice that come after our stores of grain and corn. Some farmers will even encourage this association by installing special "owl doors" to invite owls into their barns. Wherever · they hunt, owls help to keep rodent populations in check.

In New York State, the barn owl is declining in numbers because the old barns it likes to nest in are increasingly rare. Out west, barn owls have been put to work. In California's Central Valley, farmers tending almond orchards have recruited barn owls to help solve their problem with gophers. It turns out that gophers, who can damage and even kill the almond trees by chewing on the bark, are the barn owl's favorite prey. Owls released into the almond orchards have become part of an integrated pest management program, reducing the need to poison the gophers. Teenagers in local schools build nesting boxes for the owls from scrap plywood and sell the boxes to farmers, raising money for scholarships. Other creatures in the environment—including humans—are protected from exposure to poisonous pesticides. The almond trees thrive. Everybody wins—except, of course, the gophers.

There are over two hundred different species of owls, and they can be found almost everywhere on earth, from the arctic to the tropics. The tiny elf owl, only six inches tall, lives in Mexico and eats mainly insects. The burrowing owl, less than a foot tall, lives underground in tunnels abandoned by other animals. One of the largest owls, the great horned owl, grows to be nearly two feet tall, with a wingspan of over forty inches. Only the snowy owl, found in the extreme northern regions of the United States and in Canada, is larger, with a wingspan 115 of fifty-two inches. The great horned owl can be found over most of North America, and its hooting is the sound we most associate with owls. Various other species of owls can also screech, scream, whistle, whinny, bark, and hiss.

It is most likely the great horned owl that I have seen several times at our cabin—a large brown shape that swooped down from its perch in a spruce tree by the pond and flew off into the woods when I came too close on a summer's day. Only a moment before, it was invisible, blending silently into the shadows. With its layers of feathers that are like a warm down coat worn all year round, the great horned owl doesn't have to fly south in the winter, but it doesn't care much for summer's heat, so it probably found the evergreen grove Bill planted by the pond a nice, cool place to roost during the day—at least until I came along and disturbed its solitary slumber. This is owl country; great horned owls are common in New York State, although their skill at staying camouflaged helps them go unnoticed most of the time. But I know they are especially fond of the mixed evergreen and deciduous woods of an area like this, and our hayfield and the marsh at one end of the pond make this place a happy hunting ground. There are plenty of mice and voles, squirrels, chipmunks, rabbits, and even skunk for owls to prey on. It's thought owls have little or no sense of smell, because the skunk's odorous spraying does not defend them against owls. Either that, or the owls just don't care. And there are plenty of trees. There are oak trees and maple trees, pine trees and tamarack trees, spruce trees and hemlock trees, evergreen trees to provide shelter all year and tall, dead tree trunks with cavities where owls like to make their nests.

I have not seen the nest of the great horned owl, but on summer evenings, when dusk falls slowly like a long, sweet adagio and the moon rises over the hill, I have heard its muffled call of "who, who, who, who" coming to me from deep in the woods. And like Thoreau I rejoice that there are owls. "I love to hear their wailing," he wrote in *Walden*, "their doleful responses, trilled along the woodside, reminding me sometimes of music and singing birds, as if it were the dark and fearful side of music, the regrets and sighs that would fain be sung." Compared to the cheerful chirpings and coloratura arpeggios of other birds, perhaps the owl's song does sound doleful to some, but I find it soothing. When darkness descends, and I hear the owl call softly from the ancient pines on the hill, I know that I am really not alone.

In the evergreen forests of the Pacific Northwest lives another type of owl—one so solitary that few people have ever seen one. Those who have tend to describe it in rather disparaging terms. The northern spotted owl, they say, is "an unassuming bird," with "nondescript, drab plumage," in size "little bigger than a crow." Yet when I finally see a northern spotted owl up close, I find it anything but drab. Chenoa, a twelve-year-old female, was the product of an experimental breeding program intended to boost the numbers of spotted owls by placing chicks in nests where they could be adopted by wild birds. Spotted owls are notoriously slow breeders, producing few young of their own. To make matters worse, unsustainable logging over the past one hundred years had been shrinking their habitat of old-growth forests in the Pacific Northwest, and the numbers of spotted owls were declining so rapidly that by 1989 the Fish and Wildlife Service concluded that the northern spotted owl should be placed on the endangered species list.

Unfortunately, Chenoa wasn't adopted in the wild, and she was found starving, unable to fend for herself in the forest. So she was brought here to the Cascades Raptor Center in Eugene, Oregon, where she is very popular. I am only the latest of a number of human beings who have adopted her, helping to pay for her care and feeding.

She shows no signs of starvation now, but despite being almost a foot tall, she seems to have the magical ability to disappear before my very eyes. The white spots on her chocolate brown feathers are perfectly designed to mimic the dappled light in an old-growth forest of Douglas fir. Her large, deep brown eyes are liquid, surrounded by a facial disk of feathers so fine as to seem a product of the imagination—brush strokes made by smoke. Silvery rays emerge in the feathers above her eyes, like moonbeams. Even here at the Raptor Center, she blends into the greenery planted around the cages as she perches on the leather glove of Erica Broderick, the Center's Education Coordinator. The spotted owl's habit of quietly sitting also helps it to mysteriously disappear. Erica tells me that the spotted owl is a "sit and wait" predator, perching high in a tree and waiting for prey like a flying squirrel to come along before it swoops down for the kill. True forest dwellers, spotted owls require large territories of a thousand acres or more. They are not communal, they do not migrate, and they are reluctant to cross clear cuts or roads in order to hunt. They stay in the deep forest. With such a penchant for solitude, I doubt if they relish all the notoriety they have achieved. But as Erica says, "It's hard to know what an owl is thinking."

The spotted owl first came to public attention in the early 1990s, when environmentalists seized on the owl's fondness for the deep woods as a way to halt logging of old-growth forests in Washington, Oregon, and California. There is no law to protect endangered forests. The Endangered Species Act of 1973, however, provided a way to protect habitat where an endangered species lives. The spotted owl was endangered. The spotted owl's habitat was old-growth forest. Therefore, old-growth forest must be protected. This was the reasoning behind lawsuits filed by environmental groups seeking to place the spotted owl on the endangered list and halt timber sales in old-growth forests.

For the first time, the Forest Service was forced to examine the issue of habitat conservation as it related to logging, and hire biologists to prowl the woods for owls and their nests, trying to establish how much territory and what kind the spotted owl needed in order to survive. In May 1990, a Forest Service biologist named Jack Ward Thomas issued an interagency report recommending 7.7 million acres of forest in the three states be set aside for spotted owl habitat, almost half of it prime timberland scheduled for logging.

A "war in the woods" ensued between timber companies, the Forest Service, and environmental groups. The June 25, 1990, cover of *Time* magazine featured a dark, scary-looking illustration of a spotted owl with the headline "Who Gives a Hoot?" In smaller type, a subtitle read, "The Timber industry says that saving this spotted owl will cost 30,000 jobs. It isn't that simple." The unassuming, reclusive spotted owl had struck fear into the heart of an entire industry and those who depended on it for a livelihood. Logging companies feared loss of revenue, loggers feared loss of jobs, and the Forest Service itself, influenced by the logging companies, resisted the findings of the Thomas Report, insisting that timber sales continue and filing their own lawsuits objecting to the spotted owl conservation areas.

In 1992, a federal district court judge in Seattle named William Dwyer issued a permanent injunction against logging in areas of spotted owl habitat. Angry loggers began hanging spotted owls in effigy during demonstrations in towns like Forks, Washington, on the Olympic Peninsula, where logging had long been a way of life. The nondescript little bird became a symbol of the distress many people in the Northwest felt over what was rapidly becoming an endangered way of life.

But as the *Time* magazine headline suggested, the spotted owl was not entirely to blame for the distress. The logging industry had been in decline long before the spotted owl controversy. For too many years, too many old-growth trees had been cut too quickly to allow the forest to regenerate. Employment in the logging industry had already dropped drastically during the post-war period when there were few laws protecting the environment. Given free rein to cut as much of the forest as they liked, logging companies had cut as much as they could until there was little left to cut and send to sawmills. Mechanization at sawmills and the practice of exporting logs to Japan for quick profit were also costing the industry jobs. So the movement to save the spotted owl may have actually saved the logging industry by protecting the forests.

The jobs vs. owls debate gained even more national attention in the 1992 presidential election. The first President Bush supported the timber industry and opposed protection of the spotted owl with the famous saying "We'll be up to our neck in owls and out of work for every American." His opponent, Bill Clinton, pledged to find a compromise. When Clinton was elected, he and Vice President Al Gore organized a Forest Summit in Portland to bring representatives of both sides together. The result was the Northwest Forest Plan of 1994, which stopped logging in a patchwork of old-growth forests, but not everywhere. The plan allowed timber companies to continue logging trees, but not at the level they had in the past. Neither side was happy with the compromise, and the courts have been busy with 119 lawsuits ever since.

In the meantime, towns like Forks, Washington, on the edge of Olympic National Park, and Oakridge, Oregon, in the Willamette National Forest thirty miles from Eugene, have tried to reinvent themselves as tourist destinations. The descendants of loggers have built motels and restaurants and opened stores selling outdoor gear for the increasing number of urbanites in the Pacific Northwest who value opportunities for camping, hiking, fishing, and just enjoying the forest environment. Some former loggers have taken advantage of retraining money made available in Clinton's Northwest Forest Plan, and found jobs in health care, education, or the new high tech sector of the economy. Some have simply moved away. In the end, net job loss has been only about a third of the thirty thousand once predicted at the beginning of the "war in the woods."

The truth is that the debate over owls vs. jobs wasn't really about either owls or jobs; it was about forests, specifically the old-growth forests of the Pacific Northwest. Old growth had been decimated in the east, and it was nearly gone in the west. On the Olympic Peninsula in Washington, on the slopes of the Cascades in Oregon, and in the forests hugging the California coast, old growth was making its last stand. There was no other way to protect it, either in national forests, which regularly sell timber to logging companies, or on private lands where unsustainable logging was stripping it away. Illegal logging had even been discovered in remote regions of Olympic National Park. Old growth needed an advocate, and more than one environmentalist has said that if the spotted owl hadn't existed they would have had to invent it. And fortunately for the environmentalists, the spotted owl has a special liking for the cool, dark, damp conditions in an old-growth forest of Douglas fir, one of the world's most valuable and sought-after trees.

The state tree of Oregon, Douglas fir was once called "Oregon Pine" because it resembled the huge white pine that had made so many fortunes in the east. Like white pine, Douglas fir (named after the Scottish botanist David Douglas, who collected its seed on his 1825 trip to the Pacific Northwest) will only grow in open sunlight as a "pioneer tree" on burned-over, well-drained sites with deep, fertile soil where it has no competition from other trees. In such places it often forms pure stands of stately trees that grow hundreds of feet tall and many feet in diameter. The great size, strength, and mass of Douglas fir made it the timber of choice for structural beams, floors, and ceilings in the largest buildings. Douglas fir was cut to make telephone poles, railroad ties, and bridges. Second-growth Douglas fir also makes high-grade plywood because its veneer is superior in strength to that of other woods.

Cultivated, Douglas fir is a favorite for Christmas tree farms because its needles stay fresh long after the tree is cut. In the wild, the tree can live to be a thousand years old. An old-growth forest of Douglas fir has one of the largest biomasses of any type of ecosystem. The colossal old trees store enormous amounts of carbon, combating global climate change for human habitations that might be thousands of miles away. So the remaining forests of valuable old-growth Douglas fir provide humans with a decidedly practical benefit, especially as countries around the globe come to agreement about our responsibilities to protect the world's climate.

Douglas fir does not regenerate itself easily in old-growth stands, however. In the shade of towering Douglas fir, hemlock and red cedar grow up instead. In the open sunlight of clear cuts, timber companies replant with Douglas fir seedlings to take the place of the old trees. But it would be hundreds of years before these plantations would acquire the unique qualities of an old-growth forest, if they ever got the chance. In forty or fifty years, the valuable Douglas fir would be cut again.

The spotted owl prefers the dim, green groves of the old growth, where the Douglas fir is already hundreds of years old, its bark deeply furrowed and covered with moss, where hemlock and other shade-tolerant trees grow up with the fir and provide a multi-layered forest that is home to rodents like flying squirrels, one of the spotted owl's favorite prey. The dense, deep tree canopies of an old-growth forest of Douglas fir make a place called home for the spotted owl. From an ethical standpoint, we ought to consider destroying another creature's habitat wrong. "The practice of conservation must spring from a conviction of what is ethically and esthetically right," said Aldo Leopold, "as well as what is economically expedient. A thing is right only when it tends to preserve the integrity, stability, and beauty of the community, and the community includes the soil, waters, and flora, as well as people. It cannot be right, in the ecological sense, for a farmer to drain the last marsh, graze the last woods, or slash the last grove in his community, because in doing so he evicts a fauna, a flora, and a landscape whose membership in the community is older than his own, and is equally entitled to respect."

And in the needles of an old-growth Douglas fir another whole world exists, home to members of the community of life on earth that few of us even know. It is said that if the needles of only one tree were spread flat, the surface area would cover an entire football field. That surface is host to more than one team of microorganisms, a whole league of life forms that botanists have nicknamed "scuzz." Scuzz consists of microscopic bacteria, fungi, and mites, which taken together appear to form a defensive line to protect trees from predatory insects. Spiders drawn to the scuzz also help to keep insects in check, preying on intruders.

The scuzz of life in the canopy of an old-growth Douglas fir forest is a perfect example of how something we can't even see plays a part in the web of life. Is it wise to destroy something we don't yet understand? "This we know," said Chief Seattle, "the earth does not belong to man, man belongs to the earth. All things are connected like the blood that unites us all. Man did not weave the web of life, he is merely a strand in it. Whatever he does to the web, he does to himself." Honoring the multi-layered, mysterious, and sometimes even microscopic world of an old-growth forest inhabited by spotted owls is one way to affirm the truth of what Chief Seattle and Aldo Leopold said. We are all connected—man, tree, bird, even scuzz—sharing life in ways we don't yet fully understand.

❦

Despite the spotted owl's preference for the solitude of the deep woods, it doesn't seem to fear humans. Biologists who prowl the forest compiling data for the latest attempts to "delist" the owl as an endangered species and free up more old-growth forest for logging often comment on how the owl will perch on a tree branch and watch you—once you have managed to find one of the reclusive birds in the wild. Here at the Cascades Raptor Center, Chenoa sits on Erica's glove, turning her head to gaze first at Erica, and then at me. Owls have fourteen vertebrae in their necks—twice as many as humans—and because their eyes face forward and don't move around in their sockets as ours do, they have to swivel their necks to look around. No bird I've ever seen has more of the "wise old owl" look than this one. Its gaze is penetrating and calm, as if it is indeed "practicing eternity."

But I fear I may be looking into the eyes of a creature doomed to extinction. Despite the conservation areas established by the Northwest Forest Plan of 1994, the numbers of spotted owls remain in decline. Despite the hundreds of research reports produced on the spotted owl over the past twenty years, there remain many questions about the bird and its habitat. Why is the spotted owl still in trouble? It's known that larger, more aggressive barred owls are invading spotted owl territories and competing for prey, pushing out the spotted owl. It's possible that West Nile virus has also taken a toll on the spotted owl population. It's possible that the Northwest Forest Plan simply didn't go far enough in preserving old growth, or that there was already too little contiguous acreage left to meet the needs of the spotted owl. It's possible that we don't know enough to know what questions we should be asking. Meanwhile, timber companies file lawsuits to free up more land for lumbering, claiming that conservation areas haven't helped the spotted owl. The U.S. Fish and Wildlife Service has announced a new thirty-year plan for recovery of the northern spotted owl, at a projected cost of nearly half a billion dollars. The plan maintains 6.4 million acres of spotted owl conservation areas, but does nothing to restrict logging on federal lands, disappointing environmentalists.

If wisdom is the knowledge of what is good and the courage to act accordingly, as Plato said, then the question remains, who knows best what is good, the owl or humans? An owl's knowledge is one gained by the experience of living in the ancient forest, at home with the eternal mysteries of life, death, and regeneration. Human knowledge is temporal at best, often influenced by greed, politics, and the economics of short-term gains. Humans see themselves as more worthy than a forest, and more valuable than an owl. But the owl can see in the dark where we are blind. As a guardian of hidden truths, living with an instinctive knowledge of its own place in the web of life, I think the owl probably has the edge on humans, at least where eternity is concerned.

CHAPTER TEN

Impermanence

Cathedral Pines is not what it once was. It was once forty-two acres of majestic evergreens, some of them nearly three hundred years old. It was once the Northeast's tallest forest, with pine trees soaring to heights of 170 feet and more. It was once a place so hauntingly beautiful, so infused with a sense of the transcendent, that people came here to be married, as if the forest were indeed a church. The tall, straight trunks of the magnificent old pines made a sacred space of this hillside in Connecticut, a cathedral of living, growing pillars holding up an infinite blue dome of sky.

But the sky turned black when a thunderstorm roared through this corner of northwestern Connecticut on the afternoon of July 10, 1989. The storm spawned tornadoes, funnel clouds of monster wind clawing randomly at the ridge tops. Nothing in human power could stop them, and in the space of a few short minutes, one of these tornadoes destroyed a forest that had been three hundred years in the making.

A few acres of the ancient white pine and hemlock remain standing, and while Cathedral Pines is a very different forest now, it is still beautiful, even in its uniquely altered state. Today, Cathedral Pines is a testament to change, a living monument to what Buddhists call the Great Truth of Impermanence: nothing and no one stays the same.

The earth is turning toward winter and the days growing short, but October 9 is hazy and warm. The autumnal incense of decaying leaves is in the air, dusky shades of red and gold smudging the woods along the road. As we drive up Essex Hill Road from the tiny village of Cornwall, we can see the path taken by a tornado fifteen years ago in the opened canopy of trees on the hillside. As we come closer, we spot numerous tall, grayish-white snags on the hill, ghostly reminders of the storm. Two of these snags stand near the entrance to the forest, one on either side of the road. The one to the left is twisted into a corkscrew shape, as if emulating the funnel cloud that visited so much destruction here in 1989.

There are five of us in the Volvo station wagon: my husband Bill and I, Bill's youngest daughter Kate, her husband Jason Reed, and their friend Joan Meakin. But we are really six: in her womb, Kate is carrying the ten-week-old fetus of her first child, destined to be born next spring. It is the Columbus Day weekend, and we are not the only people taking a holiday here. Next to the carved wooden Nature Conservancy sign painted with the words "Cathedral Pines," three cars are already parked in the tiny lot, and another three huddle by the side of the road on a narrow berm. Jason parks the Volvo behind a dark blue Toyota Corolla in the last available space, and we all get out to explore.

The old Appalachian Trail leads right through Cathedral Pines, so we can follow the blue-blazed trees up the hill and into the forest. To our left, we can see the tornado's trail of destruction—it cut a sharp edge along an open slope where I imagine cattle could have grazed two hnudred fifty years ago. It's thought that in colonial times this hillside was cleared of hardwood trees to make pasture. Abandoned as the settlers moved on, the cleared hillside provided fertile open ground with plenty of sunlight for white pine to seed themselves and grow. Nature abhors a vacuum; white pine rushes in to grow in old, abandoned fields where there is plenty of space and light. (At least, it did before innumerable deer browsing incessantly on tender young seedlings became a problem.) Shade-loving hemlock grow up in the shadows of the pines, along with a few oak and maple trees, and a new forest is born. Scientists studying the trees at Cathedral Pines have found two growth spurts of the evergreen trees: one in the late 1700s, and another in the early 1800s. This tells them that there may have been some logging at those times, opening the forest canopy to additional sunlight and spurring additional growth.

White pine will not grow in shade; no one really knows what provided the wide, open spaces for the growth of mighty white pine forests in other areas of the Northeast six hundred years ago, long before European settlers arrived. Were years of drought followed by an immense forest fire, an apocalypse raging across millions of acres and leaving the fertile, open fields that white pine loves to fill? Did a hurricane blow inland, felling whole forests and clearing the fields to the skies? Whatever happened was a necessary process—without death, there is no life. This is a concept so simple and so profound that only a myth can explain it. I am reminded of the Hindu God Shiva who destroys, creates, and destroys again in a never-ending cycle, beating the rhythms of life and death on his drum as he dances through eternity.

What we know for sure is that, in 1883, the Calhoun family bought this property in western Connecticut to prevent its being completely destroyed by logging. And in 1967, their descendants donated it to the Nature Conservancy, with the request that it always remain in what they called "a natural state."

Its natural state is now one of disarray. As we climb the hill, we are forced to duck under the fallen pillar of an enormous tree which has been left lying right across the trail, evidence that the Nature Conservancy took the pledge to leave Cathedral Pines in "a natural state" very seriously. Tree trunks lie everywhere, "like fallen heroes," Bill says. Stripped of their bark and branches, broken and splintered, they litter the rocky slope of the hill. Some lie in piles, one on top of another, evidence of the way one tree took three or four others with it as it fell. Looking at them, I imagine I can almost hear the ominous freight-train roar of the twister and its black wind as it tore up the hillside on a summer afternoon. Now, I look down at a serene mosaic of yellowed pine needles and dried brown oak leaves, twigs, branches, and shattered strips of bark on the ground at my feet. Pine cones lie scattered about; ferns grow among mossy rocks; the ravaged, rotting branches of the fallen trees sprout white, yellow, and red fungi.

I pause to let Bill, Jason, Joan, and Kate go ahead of me, and quickly snap a photograph of them all as they walk single file up the hill. Someday, I think, Kate might bring her first child here, and say, "You were here once before, while you were still growing inside of me, waiting to be born. Do you remember?" She'll have the photograph as proof.

127

We pass a tree that looks like it has fallen only in the past year, its trunk covered in bark made emerald green by moss, its roots still roped to the soil that clings to them. In a few years, the mass of roots and soil will collapse and make a mound, leaving beside it a pit in the ground where the tree's root ball once grew. Eventually, the tree trunk itself will break down into nitrogen, feeding the soil where it lies. In the meantime, insects will feed on the trunk, and woodpeckers eat the insects. This is the way a tree dies, exchanging its life with other life, surrendering to the cycle of birth, death, and regeneration known to every forest. In its natural state, a forest does not hide its dead, or bury them. And it does not forget them. It embraces them, watching over them as they slowly return every atom of their being to the forest, becoming one with it once more in a process that I find beautiful, even enviable. It is a form of immortality, this giving back of life for more life. As long as it continues, the forest never really dies.

Nature Conservancy officials made the decision not to clear or salvage the fallen trees after the 1989 storm, despite the protests of some local citizens who were horrified at what they called the "terrible mess" of broken trees left by the storm. Some people lamented the loss of revenue that harvesting the fallen trees could provide—as much as a million board feet of straight-grained, old-growth pine, an almost incalculable sum. Others wanted to clean up the mess and replant white pine in order to try to recreate the forest for future generations to enjoy again some day. The writer Michael Pollan, who lived nearby, advocated a kind of "gardening ethic" for the preservation of Cathedral Pines, one giving humans a central role. Most likely, humans had already created Cathedral Pines by clearing the hillside in the first place, Pollan argued in his book *Second Nature*; people could make the choice to clear the dead trees now, replant white pine, and manage the forest for posterity like a well-tended garden. What he called the "wilderness ethic" of letting nature take its course without interference was an "all or nothing" proposition, leaving too many unanswered questions where a place like Cathedral Pines was concerned. Nature, he pointed out, "produces the AIDS virus as well as the rose." Entrusting a place as unique as Cathedral Pines to completely natural forces, he said, was a "hopelessly romantic" notion, at best, and at worst, it was "nihilistic."

Leaving the forest as it was after the tornado might have seemed counter-intuitive to some, but Nature Conservancy officials thought otherwise. "We're all saddened by the loss," said Leslie N. Corey, the executive director of the Nature Conservancy's Connecticut chapter, "but the area will reforest itself." Graham G. Hawks, Executive Director of the Tennessee River Gorge Trust, supported the Conservancy's decision, writing in an editorial to the *New York Times* that "the natural regeneration of the site will be a wonder to behold." Local scientists were eager to continue studying the area. Dr. Thomas Siccama, director of field studies at Yale University's School of Forestry and Environmental Studies, opposed any cleanup efforts. "It's just as pretty to me now as it was," he told the *Times*. "If you're going to clean it up, you might as well put up condos."

As a compromise, the Nature Conservancy cleared a fifty-foot-wide area of the forest from the edge of the property along the road, providing a fire break and removing the tangle of fallen trees. Here, scrub and brush has grown up, which in some ways is far less attractive than the fallen trees. Like most efforts at compromise, it has satisfied no one.

At the top of the hill, we come to the beginning of the few remaining acres of the old-growth white pine and hemlock forest, with oak and maple in among the evergreens here and there. Wind murmurs in the treetops high above us. As in any old-growth forest, there is virtually no understory; the tall, old trees long ago shaded out any others trying to grow in their shadows. Under the soaring trees, the light is muted, much as it is under the vaulted dome of a cathedral. The old white pine display the thick, corrugated, balding bark of ancient trees. A few of them are also pinned with discreetly placed little silver tags stamped with numbers. Dr. Siccama measured a permanent plot of the remaining old-growth trees at Cathedral Pines in 1990, pinning the trees to identify the points on his plot, and he follows up with new measurements every ten years. He and his students are studying the long-term growth and mortality rates of the trees in this portion of the forest.

They have also plotted the blowdown area where the forest was destroyed. One thing they have observed, Dr. Siccama has told me, is that the debris of the fallen trees has served to protect regenerating seedlings which might otherwise have been browsed off by deer. The fallen trees will take fifty to a hundred years to completely disintegrate, plenty of time to give seedlings a fighting chance against the deer.

At the far side of the hilltop we find another fallen tree, one that looks as if it was pulled into a vortex and twisted as easily as I might twist a strand of yarn. Lying still now on the ground, it was gripped in death by a violent act of nature, its bark nearly torn from its trunk. But the bark is still there, unlike that of the bare, dry trunks of the trees felled in the 1989 storm, which missed this part of the forest. This tree must have fallen a few years later.

The outrage over Cathedral Pines is understandable because to many people this place represented the equivalent of a church—a sacred, inviolable place. But sacred is not necessarily unchangeable. I can also appreciate Michael Pollan's wish to try to preserve the beauty of Cathedral Pines for future generations. Anyone who has tended a garden, as he has, knows the joy of watching what he has planted flourish. But even without tornadoes, an old-growth forest left like this in its "natural state" is never as neat and clean as a well-tended garden. It wouldn't have been that way before the 1989 storm, and it isn't now. Trees are felled by wind, or they are struck by lightning. Even in the area of old-growth forest not destroyed by the tornado here at Cathedral Pines, we find a spot where lightning has left its mark, blasting apart an ancient hemlock to leave shattered limbs and pieces of bark everywhere on the ground, just like the tree I saw at Cook Forest. Each blasted bit, Native American people say, is holy, touched by the supernatural, the all-powerful gods of thunder and lightning.

I pick up a shard of the blasted bark to examine it. About four inches long, two inches wide, and an inch thick, it fits easily in my hand. It is made of dozens of layers of paper-thin bark, rich brown and glazed with green mosses. Unlike the old-growth pine bark with its long, shaggy strips, this bark is built up in petalled plates, one on top of the other. For centuries, perhaps, it was a piece of the hemlock's only skin, protecting the tree from birds and insects, cold and ice, rain and snow. I wonder how high it was on the tree, whether wind swirled over its surface, far from where it has fallen. Once it was only a few inches somewhere on a tree with swooping branches carrying rows of short, soft green needles, spring, summer, winter, and fall, the tree we call in our language the eastern hemlock. The wind perhaps called it by a different name—something graceful, something green. Blasted apart by a bolt of lightning, it casts no shadow now. But in this piece of bark, I can still conjure the image of the tree that once stood here.

From here the trail leads downhill again, into a deep ravine. We pick our way down the slope, zigzagging across and down, across and down again to the bottom, where it looks as if a stream must run in spring. Mossy rocks fill the narrow valley. Just above the streambed a giant white pine is growing among the rocks, its bark rough and shaggy. Kate and I climb up on the rocks and stretch our arms around it to measure it, estimating a circumference of twelve feet. Jason, the engineer, helps us do the math—chest high, the trunk of this tree is nearly four feet in diameter. I cannot see its top, probably at least one hundred fifty feet above me.

"Mighty" is the only word for such a tree. It has claimed this spot in this valley for over a hundred years now, growing ever wider and ever taller. Its roots find water and minerals in the stream bed; its long green needles, somewhere high above me in another world, find the sun and the air, making food for the tree to grow the inner layers of its wood, the cambium, the sapwood, expanding outward year by year. Deep inside, the older sapwood dries and grows hard, becoming the precious heartwood that gives the tree its strength. It is difficult to resist the impulse to anthropomorphize such a tree. A tree like this suggests the presence of a philosopher king in the forest, a ruler who has the wisdom to work with universal forces; this valley is its domain. Touching this tree is like doing *darshan*, the Hindu practice of gaining blessings by touching the feet of a great and holy being who has attained the status of a saint. But even saints and kings eventually die. *131* When this tree falls, it will block the streambed and possibly change the character of the entire valley. I doubt that I will live to see it happen. But someday, it will happen.

Our group disperses as we climb up the other side of the ravine. Kate and Joan find a large, flat boulder they decide to call "the tomb." Both theater people, they think of staging a scene here, and Joan tries it out, lying on the rock, her hands clasped on her chest like the carved-stone tomb figures from the Middle Ages I have seen in Europe's Gothic cathedrals. At the top of the hill, Bill and I find the remnants of an old stone wall, and the rotted posts that must once have been a gate. The wall must be early nineteenth century, postdating colonial times, but predating the Calhoun family's purchase of the property. Its smaller stones are gradually tumbling from the boulders they were placed on to make a barrier for someone's livestock, a marker for someone's temporal ownership. Beyond are woods that are obviously much younger, beech and oak that must have grown up after logging. Jason has wandered off alone down an old logging road. We call him back.

The light has changed, and as we work our way down to the streambed and up the other side, hikers who have come from further in the woods pass us, offering greetings and heading towards the road. Back at the top of the hill, among the old-growth pines, I linger, watching the sun slip down between the pillars of the trees to slant in golden rays to the forest floor.

In our own cathedrals, we try to imitate the grandeur of nature. We even try to replicate the features of growth and light we worshipped once in ancient forests. We score marble pillars with lines imitating the bark of tall, straight trees, and top them with carved capitals imitating the leafy crowns of trees. Stained-glass windows let in shafts of muted light to fall among the pillars; the images painted in blue, red, and gold on the windows tell sacred stories of angels and saints, the birth of a savior, the wise men following a star to bring him gifts.

Here in the forest, the trees tell their own sacred stories of life, death, and transformation. Something is dying here, they tell me, and at the same time, something is alive. The dead are still among us if we look, not as spirits in the shadows but in the miracle of regeneration that lifts a growing seedling towards the light. And even in the path of death and destruction, something is waiting to be born.

As we start back down the hill to the parking lot, Bill stops and bends down to peer at the ground. "Well, look at that," he says, pointing his walking stick at a seedling no more than two inches tall. Down on the carpet of brown oak leaves, yellowed pine needles, and fallen twigs at our feet, his sharp eyes have picked out a few clusters of feathery green fronds that are unmistakably white pine. Michael Pollan worried that, left to itself, the ancient pine and hemlock forest would be succeeded not by more evergreens, but by oak, changing what was Cathedral Pines forever. I did see oak seedlings among the fallen pine trees. But here at least is proof that there may also be more pine on the way.

Cathedral Pines is not what it once was. We cannot know what it will be a hundred years from now because we won't be around to see it. We can only be sure of what it is today. Once, it stood as a monument to grandeur and serenity. Now it is a lesson in impermanence: no one and nothing stays the same. Not a human being, not a tree, and not a forest.

CHAPTER ELEVEN
Winter's Tale

The beauty of the woods in winter is in their stillness. No leaves rustle; there is only the stirring of evergreen boughs that bend in the wind, and the clouds of snow they scatter, silent crystalline songs. Warblers have left the deep woods; the hawk is circling quietly in its high kingdom. Turtle, frog, and toad sleep, burrowed in blankets of mud beneath the pond. Bat, bear, and groundhog sleep, curled up in crevices and caves. Cloaked in his warm, brown feathers, the great horned owl hunts far afield for his prey, and every night Orion shoots his arrow into the dark. These are the desperate, hungry hours, barren of fragrance, stripped of flowering warmth, shining and still in the light of the long night moon.

Dawn comes late and dusk is early; in between, at the time of the winter solstice, nine hours of daylight, barely enough, it would seem, to keep the woods and its creatures alive. Even at noon, the sun is so low in the sky that the light is crepuscular, and shadows lie long on the pure white page of the snow. The heart of life beats slow, slow as the stately pace of an old English carol written about a medieval Bohemian king:

> Good King Wenceslas looked out
> On the feast of Stephen
> When the snow lay round about
> Deep and crisp and even.

Wenceslas went out on the day after Christmas to give alms to the poor. We have come to our cabin on the first day of winter to cut a few boughs of fir for our house in town and to scatter corn and sunflower seeds for the winter birds—juncos and chickadees, cardinals and mourning doves. With children and grandchildren scattered now around the country, far from what was once home, Christmas isn't what it used to be. There's no house full of guests, no pile of presents under a tree. But here, we find other gifts awaiting us. Walking in to the cabin, we find the tracks of wild turkey, a scratchy, spiral dance I wish I could have seen, and the punctuation marks of deer hooves in the snow. Snow laps over the field, an insulating blanket. Snow is good for the ground, making a cover that closes in geothermal heat to warm the roots of trees as they wait out winter. Come spring, the snowmelt will nourish new life.

And even now, between the snow and the ground is a layer of air known as the *subnivian space*, meaning "under the snow," where heat rising from the ground melts the snow away from itself, creating a crawl space for life. Here, in a few millimeters between the crusty dome of the snow and the ground, is a place where spiders, mites, and microscopic bacteria live, ignoring the cold, working all winter at breaking down the debris of summer into fertile humus on the forest floor. This is the winter's tale: without winter, there is no summer. Without darkness, there is no light. Each moment is a gift, each breath a miracle, each day a new beginning.

❧

The land around our cabin, like most of the rolling hillsides here, was once a dairy farm. Cleared for cattle, the fields surrounding the pond were once barren of trees except for an apple orchard and the ancient pines that grow on the other side of the stream. Bill has transformed the property, planting spruce, pine, and tamarack around the spring-fed pond where his grandchildren used to swim in summer. All told, spread out over a hundred acres, he planted several thousand trees. Some survived, some did not, and some have grown better than others. The spruce have grown the fastest, making dense and shady groves to screen this woodland retreat from the road. The tamarack have also grown tall, their ropy roots gripping the soil uphill from the pond.

Tamarack don't mind having their feet wet; this muddy, spring-fed slope is just to their liking.

On either side of the stream that winds through the property Bill planted willows to hold the banks against the torrents of spring. He also planted a grove of balsam fir, living Christmas trees prized for their perfectly pointed, conical shapes, their lush green branches, and their magically calming scent. A fir, when cut, does not drop its needles as some evergreens will do, and even without watering, balsam fir boughs stay fresh for weeks, making them a favorite of wreath makers. But long before anyone thought of Christmas, with its evergreen wreaths and its Christmas trees strung with electric lights and metallic tinsel, the fir tree was sacred to Odin, wisest of the gods who ruled the fabled mountains and forests of Norseland.

In northern Europe, evergreen trees were venerated as symbols of everlasting life. When the farmer's field lay covered in snow and the orchard stripped of fruit, the evergreen offered hope that something could survive. Taller than men, miraculously alive and beautiful under frigid, starry skies, spruce and fir cast mysterious spells on the winter landscape. It's no wonder ancient people thought gods resided in these trees. What but divine presence could explain their vigor and beauty at the time of year when nothing else is green? What but great wisdom could account for their longevity? Once, the oldest and largest trees were left where they were, revered as holy beings. Once, we came to the woods to find evidence of the sacred. Bill and I still come to the woods he planted, even in winter, looking for signs of life.

Below the cabin, whiteness has covered the pond and stilled its ripples. No green and blue dragonflies hover here now, and the blue-crested kingfisher we watch for in summer will find no breakfast here today; I hope he has left for climes where ponds like this one aren't covered with ice and snow. Instead of the kingfisher, or the green herons that perch in the trees overlooking the pond on summer afternoons, we find tree sparrows, small beads of life among the branches of the tamarack trees. True messengers of winter, these brown-feathered birds with their somber gray breasts and the jaunty stripes of black and white on their wings migrate here from the boreal forests of Canada. They must be hunting for seeds among the tamarack and the dry brown weeds and grasses around the pond. Compared to the frozen, wind-swept tundra in the north, these woods must be a winter haven.

Bill spies a pair of dark gray voles running for the entrance to their burrow under a piece of pipe he left beside the path. These meadow mice make tunnels where they hide from predators and cache their stores of food. Their incessant underground excavation infuriates landscapers and gardeners—tunneling ruins the smooth emerald surface of suburban lawns and damages the ground of an orchard. The meadow mice, when they proliferate unchecked, also get into the farmer's stores of grain. Here, they sometimes get into our cabin in winter, looking for food and water we might have left behind.

As we walk down the hill, I see that the stream is laid with a white cloth of snow, its trickle of water stilled to a whisper. A few black-capped chickadees weave their wobbly way in the pines. Picking our way across the tumble of rocks in the runoff from the pond, we find the tracks of deer along the bank. Then, in a clearing, I see a spot where a skunk that must have left its winter den to look for food was challenged—by a coyote? A raccoon? Someone's unfortunate dog? The encounter was recent, perhaps late last night, leaving the skunk's odorous yellow stain on the snow. By tomorrow, all sign of the conflict will be covered in freshly fallen snow. Already, I think, the skunk will have crept back into its den somewhere nearby and fallen asleep, forgetting, curled in its black and white blanket of fur, that anything had given it reason to fight.

For now, at least, the woods are giving us peace. Fallen logs and the standing snags of limbless dead trees are giving shelter to squirrels, woodpeckers, mice, and owls. There must be dens for rabbits and foxes here, too—I see the tracks of these animals in the snow. And by the stream, the leafless gray branches of a wild apple tree are full of small, reddish brown fruit. Like Eve, I am tempted, and seeing no serpent nearby, I decide it's safe to pick one of the apples. The skin is leathery to the touch, but when I bite into the apple, it bursts in my mouth with a sweet, cold juice. All through the long, warm autumn we enjoyed this year, the fruit must have ripened, hanging on the tree. When the temperature dipped past zero earlier this month the apple froze and turned brown. After the cold spell broke, and the temperature rose, the frozen juices within the apple must have thawed, leaving this ice-cold, honeyed wine for me to sip, and the soft golden flesh that tastes like an apple baked in ice. Only a unique sequence of days when the air by the stream was first warm, then cold, then very cold, and finally rising to just over the freezing mark could have created this unusual fruit. I doubt any human science could reproduce it. It is truly a gift of the moment, never to come again. I pick two more of the small brown apples and stash them in my pocket, but I know they won't taste as good at home as they do right here, eaten in the fresh, cold air of the woods by the snow-covered stream.

Ten yards away are the balsam fir Bill planted thirty years ago. They reach for the sky with their pointed tops, their lower branches spreading out wide near the ground, making a sheltering space for deer. The deer also come here to rub their antlers against the fir tree's smooth outer bark. The bark on one of the trees is rubbed raw, leaving a ragged orange wound. The tree's skin cannot heal itself over as ours would do, but come spring, the new growth of wood will gather itself around the wound, the bark making ridges protecting the tree as well as it can from invading insects and mold. Many of the fir trees have these buckled scars, a sign of too many deer traversing the woods, despite the hunters that Bill has allowed to come here through the years.

The tree sparrows have followed us, flitting about in the branches of balsam fir. Bill locates a tree that is lush and full, growing in a spot where it has found more light and water than the rest. Once, it was a tiny seedling he held in his hands and placed in a cleft of soil. Now, it towers over us, fifty feet tall or more. Without ever having been trimmed, it has grown into a shapely green cone with branches that brush the sky. This is the type of tree that inspired the German carol "O Tannenbaum" for *tanne* means fir. The original German words sing the fir tree's praises, calling it wondrously "loyal" (*treu*) because its leaves (*blatter*) stay green not only in summer time, but also in winter, when it snows (*wenn es schneit*).

139

> O Tannenbaum, O Tannenbaum
> Wie treu sind deine Blatter!

O Tannenbaum, O Tannenbaum,
Wie treu sind deine Blatter!
Du grunst nict nur
Zur Sommerzeit
Nein auch im Winter, wenn es schneit
O Tannenbaum, O Tannenbaum,
Wie treu sind deine Blatter!

We are hoping the balsam fir Bill has planted here so close to the southern limit of its range is not only loyal, but also forgiving, because we want some of its lovely green *blatter* to decorate our home. Bill thinks this tree looks healthy enough to spare us a branch, and with the long-handled trimming tool he has carried with him on our walk, he reaches up to locate one in the densest part of the tree where we hope it won't be missed, and cuts it neatly away. The tree seems to shiver; the branch falls into our waiting hands, green and fragrant and surprisingly large. We cut it into several pieces and sling them over our shoulders, heading back up the hill to the pond, following paths the deer have made in the snow. All the while, I breathe in the scent of balsam resin oozing from the cut bough I carry. This is the legendary balm of Gilead, a precious perfume from the Holy Land that could calm all fears, erase the memory of hurt, and still the storm of anger, replacing it with peace and joy. The magical scent is manufactured now, added to candles and air fresheners and potpourri for holiday consumption. As I walk up the hill, I have it free for the taking, a gift of the green, and I hope, forgiving tree.

As we head for the road past the apple orchard, finding our own deep tracks in the snow, a downy woodpecker busies itself in the highest branches of one of the gnarled old trees. Blue jays are screeching—I cannot see them, somewhere deep in the spruces, but I recognize their complaining calls. The blue jay is one bird that doesn't honor the quiet time of winter. When we reach the road we see a pair of mourning doves in flight, their fluttering wing beats a benediction. High overhead, in a milky sky, snow clouds are forming. We load the fragrant fir boughs into the trunk of the car and point ourselves toward home.

140

Resources and References

PLACES

I hope that all of you who read this book will seek out forests both large and small to visit in your own areas of the country. To visit any of the places profiled in this book, you can use the following contact information. Most of the Web sites will provide you with directions.

Cook Forest State Park
P.O. Box 120
Cooksburg, PA 16217
814-744-8407
www.dcnr.state.pa.us

DeVeaux Woods State Park
Niagara Frontier Region
P.O. Box 1132
Niagara Falls, NY 14303
716-284-4691
www.nysparks.state.ny.us/parks

Sprague's Maple Farms
1048 Route 305
Portville, NY 14770
716-933-6637
800-446-2753
www.spraguesmaplefarms.com
For other maple producers open during sugaring season in New York, visit www. mapleweekend.com

Great Smoky Mountains National Park
Park Headquarters
107 Park Headquarters Road
Gatlinburg, TN 37738
865-436-1200
www.nps.gov/grsm

Yosemite National Park
Public Information Office
P.O. Box 577
Yosemite, CA 95389
209-372-0200
www.nps.gov/yose/

Allegheny National Forest
Forest Headquarters
222 Liberty Street
Warren PA 16365
814-723-5150
www.fs.fed.us/r9/forest/allegheny/

Letchworth State Park
Park Headquarters
One Letchworth State Park
Castile, NY 14227
585-493-3600
www.nysparks.com

Glen Iris Inn
7 Letchworth State Park
Castile, NY 14427
585-493-2622
www.glenirisinn.com

Olympic National Forest
Forest Headquarters
1835 Black Lake Boulevard SW
Olympia, WA 98512
www.fs.fed.us/r6/Olympic/

Pacific Ranger Station
353 South Shore Road
P.O. Box 9
Quinault, WA 98575
360-288-2525

Cascades Raptor Center
32275 Fox Hollow Road
P.O. Box 5386
Eugene, OR 97405
541-485-1320
www.eRaptors.org

Cathedral Pines
Essex Hill Road
Cornwall, CT 06753

*For more information about Cathedral
Pines, contact*
**The Nature Conservancy,
Connecticut Chapter**
55 High Street,
Middletown, CT 06457
860-344-0716

REFERENCES FOR FURTHER READING

Adams, Jonathan S. *The Future of the Wild: Radical Conservation for a Crowded World*. Boston: Beacon, 2006.

Armstrong, Karen. *A Short History of Myth*. Edinburgh, Scotland: Canongate Books Ltd., 2005.

Berry, Thomas. *The Dream of the Earth*. San Francisco: Sierra Club Books, 1988.

Brower, Kenneth. "The Proof is in the Pellet: Students in California's Central Valley Have All Spotted Evidence that the Barn Owls They Raise and Release Feast in Neighboring Fields."*Audubon*. March 2004: 79-83.

Carson, Rachel. *Silent Spring*. Boston: Houghton Mifflin, 1962.

Cook, Anthony. *The Cook Forest: An Island in Time*. Helena, MT: Falcon Press, 1997.

Cooper, Susan Fenimore. *Rural Hours*. 1850. Syracuse, NY: Syracuse University Press, 1968.

Dietrich, William. *The Final Forest: The Battle for the Last Great Trees of the Pacific Northwest*. New York: Simon and Schuster, 1992.

Duncan, James. *Owls of the World: Their Lives, Behavior, and Survival*. Buffalo, NY: Firefly Books, 2003.

Egan, Timothy. "Oregon Thrives as it Protects Owls." *American Forests*, Jan/Feb 1995: 13+

Guglielmino, Janine. "More Owls is Not Equal to Fewer Jobs." *American Forests*, Summer, 1997: 6+.

Gup, T. "Owl vs. Man." *Time*. 25 June 1990: 56+.

Hartesveldt, R. J., H.T. Harvey, H. S. Shellhammer, and R. E. Stecker. *Giant Sequoias*. Three Rivers, CA: The Sequoia Natural History Association: 1981.

Heinrich, Bernd. *The Trees in My Forest*. New York: Harper Collins, 1997.

Kershner, Bruce, and Robert Leverett. *The Sierra Club Guide to the Ancient Forests of the Northeast*. San Francisco: Sierra Club Books, 2004.

Kirk, Ruth. *The Olympic Rain Forest: An Ecological Web*. Seattle: University of Washington Press, 1992.

Lawrence, James, and Rux Martin. *Sweet Maple*. Montpelier: Vermont Life, 1993.

Leopold, Aldo. *A Sand County Almanac*. New York: Oxford University Press, 1949.

Muir, John. *The Yosemite*. New York: The Century Company, 1912.

Nhat Hanh, Thich. *The Long Road Turns To Joy: A Guide to Walking Meditation.* Berkeley: Parallax Press, 1996.

Niemi, Ernie, Ed Whitelaw, and Elizabeth Grossman. "Bird of Doom ... Or Was It?" *The Amicus Journal.* Fall 2000. 22: 3. 19+.

Peattie, Donald Culross. *A Natural History of Eastern Trees.* Boston: Houghton Mifflin, 1952.

————. *A Natural History of Western Trees.* Boston: Houghton Mifflin, 1953.

Pollan, Michael. *Second Nature: A Gardener's Education.* New York: Atlantic Monthly Press, 1991.

Roszak, Theodore. *The Voice of the Earth: An Exploration of Ecopsychology.* New York: Simon and Schuster, 1992.

Scott, Doug. *The Enduring Wilderness· Protecting Our Natural Heritage Through the Wilderness Act.* Golden, CO: Fulcrum Publishing, 2004.

Seawall, Laura. *Sight and Sensibility: The Ecopsychology of Perception.* New York: Tarcher, 1999.

Swetnam, Thomas W., Ramzi Touchan, Christopher H. Baisan, Anthony C. Caprio, and Peter H. Brown. "Giant Sequoia Fire History in Mariposa Grove, Yosemite National Park." Yosemite Centennial Symposium Proceeding, "Natural Areas and Yosemite: Prospects for the Future," 1990.

Thoreau, Henry David. *Walden.* 1854. Boston: Beacon Press, 1997.

Tresidder, Mary Curry. *The Trees of Yosemite.* New York: Oxford University Press, 1932.

Turner, Jay. "Balanced Future Requires Intelligent, Bipartisan Decisions." *Erie Times News*, 25 February, 2005.

Ulrich, Roger S. "View Through a Window May Influence Recovery from Surgery." *Science*, 224:27 April, 1984: 420-21.

Williams, Ted. "Public Menace." *Audubon.* July-August 2005: 20+.

ORGANIZATIONS

The following is a short list of organizations supporting forest conservation and providing opportunities to learn more about our native forests. Contact them for information about their activities and publications.

American Forests
734 15th Street NW 8th floor
Washington, DC 20005
202-737-1944
www.americanforests.org

National Audubon Society
700 Broadway
New York, NY 10003
212-979-3000
www.audubon.org
Consult the Web site for local chapters

Eastern Native Tree Society (ENTS)
www.nativetreesociety.org
ENTS is a cyberspace interest group and discussion list devoted to celebrating the trees of Eastern North America. This free Web site has information about tall trees, notices about field trips, and a booklist.

Friends of Allegheny Wilderness
220 Center Street
Warren, PA 16365
814-723-0620
www.pawild.org

Friends of Great Smoky Mountains
National Park
P.O. Box 5650
Sevierville, TN 37864

The Nature Conservancy
4245 N. Fairfax Drive
Suite 100
Arlington, VA 22203
1-800-628-6860
www.nature.org
Consult the Web site for regional offices

Pacific Forest Trust
California Main Office
The Presidio
1001-A O'Reilly Avenue
San Francisco, CA 94129
415-561-0700
www.pacificforest.org
Consult the Web site for other state offices

Sierra Club
85 Second Street, 2nd floor
San Francisco, CA 94105
415-977-5500
www.sierraclub.org
Consult the Web site for local chapters

The Wilderness Society
1615 M Street NW
Washington, DC 20036
1-800-THE-WILD (1-800-843-9453)
www.wilderness.org
Consult the Web site for regional offices

Acknowledgements

This book could never have been written without the help of many kind and generous tree people. Dale Luthringer, Doug Bassett, Randy Sprague, Steve Marcus, and Kirk Johnson all gave of their time and made sure I found my way home. Kristine Johnson, Jim Renfro, and Glenn Taylor at Great Smoky Mountains National Park spent hours answering my questions about hemlocks. Dr. Carl Jones opened the doors of his laboratories at the University of Tennessee in Knoxville; he and Dr. Ernie Bernard and their research assistants shared with me what they know about the hemlock woolly adelgid.

Dr. Thomas Siccama of Yale University patiently answered my questions about Cathedral Pines. Louise Shimmel and Erica Broderick of the Cascades Raptor Center in Eugene, Oregon, and Ron Walker of Friends with Feathers in Avon, New York, shared with me their extensive knowledge of owls. Duncan Deschler shared his knowledge of making maple syrup.

Fred and Mary Brenner, Betty Fasnacht, Jason Reed, Kate Underhill, and John and Clem Underhill provided maps, meals, lodging, and friendship. A patient and supportive group of fellow writers (otherwise known as the Pond House writers) read each chapter and provided invaluable feedback. They are Carol Burdick, Sue Beckhorn, Cathy Engle, Lee Marcus, Kathryn Ross, and Megan Staffel. A writer couldn't ask for better friends or better readers.

During my research, my home away from home was the David Howe Memorial Library in Wellsville, New York, where I found so many of the references I consulted as well as the companionship of an attentive and friendly staff in an extraordinarily beautiful setting.

Sadly, Bruce Kershner, one of the most enthusiastic advocates of old-growth forest, succumbed to cancer before this book was completed. I have left the description of the hike he lead to DeVeaux Woods as it was written, in present tense, because his devotion to the cause of preserving even the smallest old-growth forests lives on. I am one of many people here in western New York and around the country who find it difficult to believe that he is gone.

Mary Elizabeth Braun, Acquisitions Editor at Oregon State University Press, gave her enthusiastic support to the book as it went through the process of editorial review, and I will be forever grateful for her kindness and generosity. It has been my honor to work with her and with everyone at OSU Press, especially Managing Editor Jo Alexander and Associate Director and Marketing Manager Tom Booth. The dedication of university presses has been one of the greatest blessings of my life as a writer.

I am also grateful to the Association for the Study of Literature and Environment for publishing "Impermanence" in slightly different form in the Summer 2007 issue of *ISLE* (Interdisciplinary Studies in Literature and Environment).

Finally, this book would not exist at all without the loving companionship and support of my husband Bill Underhill, who walked beside me in the woods on so many of my journeys, read the final manuscript, and shared many of his own observations and insights. His influence appears on every page. Off the page, we continue our journey through life together.

❧

Excerpts from "Sweetness always" from *Extravagaria* by Pablo Neruda, translated by Alastair Reid. Translation copyright © 1974 by Alastair Reid. Reprinted by permission of Farrar, Straus and Giroux, LLC.

Excerpt from "The Path Is You" from *The Long Road Turns to Joy: A Guide to Walking Meditation* (1996) by Thich Nhat Hanh with permission of Parallax Press, Berkeley, California, www.parallax.org <http://www.parallax.org>

Five lines from section 52 from *Tao Te Ching by Lao Tzu, A New English Version with Foreword and Notes,* by Stephen Mitchell. Translation copyright © 1988 by Stephen Mitchell. Reprinted by permission of HarperCollins Publishers